D1242416

Dear Phyllis

the
Voice
in the
Mountains

[signatures]

the Voice in the Mountains

The Abduction and Survival of Peggy Ann Bradnick

by Peggy Jackson
and Chris Armagost

Mountain Voices, LLC

Published by
Mountain Voices LLC
PO Box 147
Three Springs, PA 17264
peggyannsbook@gmail.com

10 9 8 7 6 5 4 3 2 1

First paperback edition: March 2017
Revised: July 2017
First hardcover edition: June 2017
First electronic edition: July 2017

Cover photography and design by Chris Armagost
Interior design by Chris Armagost

ISBN 978-0998781303

Library of Congress Control Number: 2017904096
Mountain Voices LLC, Three Springs, PA

To Al.

And to Mildred and Eugene Bradnick, who made sure that I could survive, and who wanted me to set the record straight.

And to the friends and family who have been wondering why something like this hasn't been done before now.

"And we know that all things work together for good to them that love God"
Romans 8:28 KJV

Introduction

by Mr. Lloyd Dell

It's not very often a person reflects on an event fifty years in the past, but this book has reflections, insights, testimony and personal accounts of a series of incidents that shook the tranquility of bucolic central Pennsylvania just over half a century ago.

In 1963 I began a career in communications that I never suspected would lead me into one of the biggest news stories this nation had experienced following the assassination of President John F. Kennedy. I started working for WHUN Radio in Huntingdon, Pennsylvania as a disc jockey.

WHUN, as well as *The Daily News* newspaper, were owned by local resident John Biddle. Some of the responsibilities that came along with being a disc jockey were both the broadcasting of local news items as well as national news stories supplied by United Press International teletype. Local news included hospital admissions and discharges, death notices, and a myriad of local gossip that rural folks would be interested in. The local information that we read was secured by various means, one of which was to go to the newspaper office and pick up carbon copies of stories to be published. We had to take them back to the radio station and condense them for our broadcast. Someone at the radio station also made daily trips to the State Police barracks to make sure anything newsworthy on their end was not overlooked.

Within a year of starting my job in the spring of 1963, a series of incidents began to occur in the southern part of Huntingdon County. These incidents were very sporadic and somewhat bizarre, not what regular local news was supposed to look like. Because of the relationship with the newsroom at the newspaper, and the rapport with the State Police, a lot of information about these incidents was kept very close to the vest. The puzzling thought was that crimes were occurring, and the perpetrator completely vanished without leaving any evidence. But who was he? Through time, he became known locally as "The Mountain Man" because he would disappear into the mountains. No vehicle, no car or conveyance could be found. Because no one could identify this individual, some thought that perhaps more than one person was involved. But with these odd incidents increasing over a two- and then three-year period, the newspaper and radio station were both wanting more information. These two entities gained the trust of the station commander of the PSP and together they discussed these incidents at length. At the time, the *Daily News* newspaper bundles were delivered throughout southern Huntingdon County and into northern Fulton County by Don Stuller, one of the radio announcers. He was among those especially asked to keep his eyes open during his travels on the rural roads.

Most of us at the radio station and newspaper worked the news beat; WHUN station manager Bill German, the *Daily News* editor

Eugene Shore, and his brother Blair Shore were keenly aware of what was happening in southern Huntingdon County. Blair Shore doubled as advertising salesperson for the radio station and the photographer for the *Daily News*. With these relationships, there were no secrets and all news was shared.

As time went on and the incidents continued, we all had our opinions and theories. The State Police had not been thoroughly convinced that one person was responsible for all of the happenings. The PSP conducted numerous interviews and talked to dozens of people, still giving them nothing concrete to go on from an investigative standpoint. Speaking with them individually and privately, every person had their own theory. Yet no single perpetrator could be identified.

All of this speculation came to a head on May 11th, 1966. A teenager, Peggy Ann Bradnick, was kidnapped by a strange-looking man after she and her siblings had gotten off the school bus and began walking home.

The news spread. Within hours this was major news and the word was spreading across central Pennsylvania. Pennsylvania State Police, news reporters, locals who had been affected by the bizarre incidents of the past few years, relatives of Peggy and total strangers began to descend on Shade Gap, Pennsylvania. The "Mountain Man" had struck again. This time he had gone way too far.

As a news gatherer I was there every day of this eight-day ordeal, sometimes officially as a news reporter, sometimes as a member of the Pennsylvania National Guard, 104th Armored Cavalry. The whole 104th was activated several days into the hunt. Other days we were there on a voluntary basis. In both capacities, I could gather information that may not always have been available to Joe Public.

I continued to work my early morning shift, "The Wake-Up Show," on WHUN Radio. We signed on at 5 a.m. and my shift ended at 8 a.m. Unbeknownst to me, by the third day of the manhunt word of the abduction had spread around the world. I started receiving calls from London and Honolulu wanting fresh reports about the progress of the search.

It didn't take long before we were asked by the FBI and PSP to stop broadcasting explicit information about the operation. We complied.

They were thinking that the perpetrator might have a radio and might be listening to our broadcasts, thus permitting the hunted to stay one step ahead of the hunters.

By the third day of the search, the local Salvation Army was looking for volunteers to deliver food and drinks from the headquarters in Huntingdon to the command post at the picnic grounds at Shade Gap. Two ladies, my recently widowed mother and her spinster sister, volunteered for the job (for those who remember, my aunt was "Old Ironsides," principal of the Mill Creek elementary school.) Both had always supported the work of the Salvation Army, and since they had a station wagon, they were qualified to make the daily trips to Shade Gap. These were always evening trips because both women taught school, and it was still mid-May.

During this whole ordeal, US Route 522 from Shade Gap to the county line was under construction. Some parts were one lane, some dirt only. These women had to deliver goods to the southern command post of the search at the Hollenbaugh cabin. With God as their protector they continued the mission, straight into the area where any action could be expected to take place.

The story comes full circle. Following Hollenbaugh's demise and Peggy's return to health weeks after, the search of the mountains began all over again. This time it was led by Peggy. The PSP, with volunteers from the Pennsylvania National Guard, scoured the mountains on weekends looking for caves and hiding places where the abductor had stashed supplies and guns. Still working for WHUN Radio and as a National Guardsman I was there on top of the story.

Over the years much has been written about the search for Peggy Ann: newspaper articles, magazine stories, and a few books. But this book gives the reader a very different viewpoint. Peggy Ann Bradnick Jackson vividly tells her story of the eight days she spent with "Bicycle Pete," *aka* "the Mountain Man," William Diller Hollenbaugh.

I hadn't talked to Peggy in fifty years, not wanting to bring up the painful past. But when I finally made contact with her, I was surprised. Peggy, through her speaking engagements and her life, shows mature Christian love exhibiting mercy and grace to all, even those like William Hollenbaugh who have wronged her through the years.

This is her account of abuse, neglect, love, mercy and forgiveness; perhaps the most compelling account ever documented in the rural central Pennsylvania mountains of Appalachia.

November 2016

Chapter 1

In the spring of 1966, I was Peggy Bradnick, seventeen years old. On May eighteenth of that year, by the grace of God, I still lived.

Most of Shade Valley, between Shade Gap and Burnt Cabins in southern central Pennsylvania, is very much the same as it was fifty years ago. I was the eldest of six children; we lived with our mother and father in a rented house half a mile or so off Pleasant Hill Road.

My mother was from the Harrisburg area, but was raised near Neelyton by Guy and Marie Price with their daughter Shirley. During the War, Mildred Louise Moore had trained to be a professional welder; but then the war ended and no one would hire a woman for a man's job anymore. She married Dad and worked at whatever she could find. While we were in school she cleaned houses, which let her set her own schedule that allowed lots of time for her family. Mom was wonderful. She cooked and baked, sang beautifully and invented games for her growing family.

My father changed his name when he volunteered during World War II. He'd never liked to be called Wayne, so he switched it with his middle name, Eugene. He went to Altoona and enlisted in the 12th Infantry, spending more than a year overseas from the spring of 1944 until 1945. He earned his Purple Heart in the Battle of the Bulge. Shot through his jaw, he spent over a year healing in the hospital.

He carried some of the same baggage home with him as many other servicemen who had seen action. He seldom spoke about his experiences, but he was plagued by alcoholism. Since Dad wasn't particularly sociable unless he went on a binge – he never imbibed at home – the neighborhood saw him as a drunk. For most of the time, though, I remember him as a good father and husband, never above doing any household chores to make things easier for Mom. He always seemed to have a broom in his hand.

"Do we have any hot dogs?" he'd ask, when everyone was home from school and work, and Mom was tired. We seldom did. Mom liked them, but he didn't really, and they cost money.

"Well then," he'd say, "I'd better cook." He was an excellent cook.

Dad had trouble keeping in work. Paying the rent was always an issue. There were lots of places for rent, and we lived in a lot of them, from Mount Union to Shade Gap, all over the southern end of the county. Money was always tight, and we were forever moving to a cheaper place. Suffice it to say that we had experience with all the variations on plumbing, sanitation, electrical and telephone service, kitchen fixtures, storage, furniture, everything. We were used to Mom looking around inside a new place, and telling us not to get too comfortable. Our lives were lived out of boxes, never quite unpacked. Once I made up a song about it:

> *Take up thy bed and walk,*
>
> *Put your things in a box,*

Doesn't matter if it's a little or a lot.

Take it with you where you go,

Put it in a safe spot.

Leave it there a little while,

Pick it up when it's time to go.

'Cause this place won't last for long,

Soon we'll pick it up, then we'll be gone.

Things weren't so bad with just myself and my brother Jim, who is a year younger than I am. Then, when I was six, Mary was born; afterward, not quite two years later, the twins Debbie and Donnie and my youngest sister Carol Jean were born within ten months of each other, giving us a toddler and three babies. Six children are expensive to raise, at best. Our housing went downhill even further after that; but I don't remember ever going hungry.

Some of the buildings are still there. For a while both Mom and Dad worked at a local nursing home, so we all lived there. The house behind the Shirley Ayr Farm dairy store is falling down, though, and the concrete store itself was torn down long ago. Mom used to send us there for fresh milk – we'd turn in the used glass bottles and get full ones, and they'd send us home with ice cream cones. For a while we lived in Pogue, between Orbisonia and Three Springs. The house had a party line for telephone service, which meant we shared a phone line with two other houses, and might have to wait for someone to hang up before we could make a call.

First grade for me was in the one-room school in Pogue, where Mrs. Kelly managed to teach every subject and control all the students in all the grades without an aide. Anyone who gave any trouble was set to work ranking firewood, shoveling snow, or whatever needed to be done. The day was tightly scheduled: every grade had its class time and its study time. The new Shade Gap Elementary School opened the following year, and is still in use.

Aside from that, I spent time at both the old red-brick Mount Union Elementary and the Shirley Township schools. Four different schools before seventh grade, some more than once.

Eventually we settled in a rented house south of Shade Gap, half a mile and more back a dirt road. It still had an outhouse and no phone, but it did have running water and electricity, and the landlord installed a new cement floor in the outhouse for us. (I'm sure we were *not* the only household in the school district to use one!) When I went out there after dark I had the four younger ones tagging along so they didn't have to go outside alone. Baths were in a tub behind the stove as water heated in every pot we had on the burners, while washing-up was from a basin carried up to the bedroom. Upstairs, all four of us girls shared the largest room in back, with my brothers across the hall and my parents in the third bedroom next to them.

We were able to have a small TV, black and white of course, with an aerial uphill by the chicken coop. Tuning in when it was windy or raining required a relay: one person outside to move the antenna, one at the TV, and someone at the door to yell instructions up the hill.

Across the lane and up a hollow, at the top of the hill, lived Grandma Goldie, Dad's mother. We went to visit often, having Mr. Frehn drop us off the school bus at her house or hiking up from our place, even through occasional hip-deep snow in winter, getting good drinking water for her from a spring along the way. Once we had settled in our house, we were there throughout my high school years, and beyond. Grandma lived near a church, and she made sure we attended regularly. We finally had a home.

Most work that Dad and Mom had was seasonal, at canneries and sawmills, but we kept chickens and maybe a beef or a few hogs, and Dad would butcher both for us and for neighbors; and there were the deer, taken only when needed. Plucking, singeing, and washing chickens for dinner was one of my least favorite chores, but if we wanted to eat it, it had to be done. We raised a vegetable garden too, and we canned everything we could. We could get our flour, sugar, salt and ketchup and so on, in the small general stores. I hardly set foot in a supermarket until after I graduated.

No matter how hard up we were, though, we were never to ask for favors or charity, nor were we allowed to take it if offered. Once, when I might have been eight or nine, Mom ran out of vanilla when she was baking. I went out onto the front porch, and had the good luck to catch the Jewel Tea man. Jewel Tea was one of the companies at the time that sold their wares door to door. I told him that my Mom was baking and had run out of vanilla. Did he have any? Yes, he did have vanilla with him that week.

Mom came out onto the porch. "No," she argued, pushing me behind her. "We can't afford to buy anything today."

There was some dickering. The salesman knew Mom. "I'm not just giving you anything, ma'am. I expect some cake the next time I come through."

Mom relented, and baked. The salesman got an entire white cake with shredded coconut on top the next time he came through, as I recall. It was only one skirmish in a long war. Every now and again, he might have some candy or something for us, and tell Mom that it was free samples or that it would go bad if he didn't unload it, or some such excuse. Mom would counter with baked or canned goods in trade.

But at the time, I had to ask: "Am I in trouble, Mom?"

"No," she sighed. "But you aren't to ask for anything like that again, understand?"

As soon as I could, I worked. Aside from chores I spent a great many of my after-school hours babysitting my brothers and sisters; later I would work for pocket money, going out to do housework or babysitting for a dollar an hour or so. I not only contributed to the household income that way, but I was able to save up enough for things like my class ring – that took five dollars a week, set aside from my earnings, for two months. It was gold with a blue stone, the school colors, with the usual Rocket mascot on one side of the stone and the graduation year on the other, and my initials on the inside. I wasn't particularly impressed with it as jewelry, but it was my class ring.

Life did not lack diversions *if* you had money, but for us they were rare treats, few and literally far between – movie theaters, skating rinks, week-long carnivals, ice cream and hot dog stands, the East Broad Top Railroad, a few community pools or state parks like Cowan's Gap, and so on.

The family liked to go to the Shade Gap Picnic, all eight of us. We'd be given perhaps fifty cents apiece to amuse ourselves, and we were expected to have a little change afterward. Dad would grumble about Mom wasting half a dollar herself, going to the fortune-teller's tent; she certainly didn't believe in that sort of thing. Once I asked her why she did it.

"Because it ticks off your Dad," she replied. Much later, I figured out that a few minutes off her feet while Dad watched us kids *was* her fortune.

For teenagers, entertainment came with friends. All it took was money, time, a ride, and permission. When I say *friends*, I do not mean a date or a boyfriend. I had neither until after my junior year. Our upbringing was strict, if nothing out of the ordinary at the time, and my parents supported one another when it came to discipline. It didn't help that puberty had hit me earlier than usual. I had that much more time in which to be told that *nobody* was to see or touch certain parts of my body until I was married to the right man; and if it wasn't the right man, I was to scream, knock him on his rear, and run. Grandma Goldie did not put it so delicately.

Even without boys to worry about, my parents were not generous with their consent, and they weren't entirely unreasonable. Mom once let me go to the Huntingdon County Fair, for instance, right around my fifteenth birthday. My friend's mother drove, and we had a nice afternoon – until it came time to go home, that is. We waited and we searched, but her mother was nowhere to be found. Finally, we found a ride with an acquaintance who took us as far as *The Hole in the Wall,* a restaurant in Mount Union. Mrs. Stoner let us use the restaurant's phone to call my friend's father. Another customer, a man whom we knew, overheard all this and offered me a ride to my house, rather than having my friend's dad go that far out of his way.

"I know your Dad from work," Mark reassured me. "He likes me. It'll be okay, Peggy."

He drove me straight home. By the time we pulled up at my house, I was a nervous wreck, shaking and crying. I didn't worry about what would happen to me, so much as what Dad might do to Mom, who had allowed me to go. Mark left me in the car for a moment to knock on the door and explain to my father what had happened. It was all right in the end. Dad accepted what we said without holding it against Mom or myself, and I was happy not to go anywhere again with my friend's mom driving.

I am still alive because of what I learned from Mom during all those years. Now and again, there were those evenings when Mom would listen for the car, waiting. When it pulled in she'd send us upstairs to bed. She'd reassure us that no matter what we heard, she'd be all right. Whatever followed when Dad came in, however loud and angry and suspicious he was after a night out at a bar, we never heard her raise her voice in anger or fear; always low-key, not confrontational. The next morning, Dad might feel guilty for her bruises, but within days or weeks there would always be the next time.

He was careful never to take out his anger on his children, and I was never afraid of him, unless I did something wrong. Then, I knew he'd blame Mom, and what he might do then *did* scare me. It took a long, long time for my own anger, over what he did to Mom all those years, to fade.

Nonetheless, Dad taught us a great deal. We respected firearms and knew how to shoot, for instance. If we were caught out in the rain, we knew to shelter under the leaves of a mountain laurel. During the years we lived in Shade Valley, he made sure we knew how to orient ourselves: we were to look for the distinctive peak of Sidney's Knob at the southern end of the valley. Any of us could have been dropped anywhere in the valley and walked home.

Practically every man, and a great many women, hunted at the time. We were not the only family with a tight budget, by any means, and venison and small game were welcome additions to the dinner table and the freezer. We were all very independent. There was no local police force, just the State Police with their Smokey Bear hats, and their presence was usually resented since it only meant trouble for someone.

Leash laws, if any, were ignored; dogs were allowed to run loose. The exception was a dog that preyed on livestock or ran deer. A single dog might not bring down a deer, but running the weight off one for fun was taking food from a youngster's mouth. Dad had to give away a good dog of his once because she chased deer.

Marksmanship and woods-craft were naturally a matter of pride. Dad got a good laugh once when my brother went up the hill one evening to adjust the TV antenna, and flushed a man from the cover of the jack pines. He'd been wearing a hunter's orange coveralls, but since he ran off into the dusk without a word, my brother didn't get any other details. The lost hunter, probably some city guy we thought, had a small load of ridicule heaped upon his unknowing head and was promptly forgotten.

I wasn't really aware at first that around the

time we settled into our house, more criminal complaints than usual began to crop up, not just in Shade Gap but all over the area. Since we didn't have a phone or a newspaper subscription, news filtered through slowly. Once the postman told us that a man had blocked Decorum Road with logs the previous evening and shot at a car, injuring a mother and her baby; but since it had happened some miles away, we weren't too concerned. We didn't have anything anyone might want back here. Most of the problems seemed to be up around Neelyton and Shade Gap anyway.

Now and again, Aunt Marie and Uncle Guy Price would ask if I could visit their house near Neelyton. Mom would consider, and say: "Peggy's been working hard lately, I suppose she can spend a night away." I visited one Friday in June or July of 1964 – I remember it was hot. The guest room had a vent screen that propped the window open. I'd gone up to bed first. My aunt and uncle were still downstairs when I heard the screen start to rattle around. The window overlooked the back addition. Its roof was nearly flat and was easily reached from the ground, so I thought it was a cat, or even a wildcat trying to get in to catch mice. I went back down and told

Uncle Guy.

"Wait down here," he ordered as he went to check. We waited. Eventually he came back in.

"It wasn't a cat," he reported. "It was a man. He ran off toward Ned's. The ladder was up against the roof outside your room." Ned Price was his brother, and a neighbor. Our branch of the family just wasn't as close to him and his wife Jessie as we were to Uncle Guy and Aunt Marie.

I slept downstairs on the couch that night. In the long run, it didn't worry us too much; there was an unlicensed bar nearby, and weekend nights often saw the customers sleeping it off on someone else's barn floor or porch, or trying to sneak into the wrong house.

Everybody heard about the little girl who went missing in March of 1965. Kathy Shea left home to walk to her elementary school a few blocks away, up in Tyrone, and hasn't been seen since. Again, though, that was over fifty miles away. It joined with the Civil Rights movement, men in orbit, Vietnam, and our own local crime wave to convince us all that the world was going mad and nowhere was safe, before we went back to the business of everyday life.

Good Friday, 1965, was also the day before

fishing season opened. While his wife was at church, Ned Price went outside after dark to dig for worms and surprised a prowler, who shot at Ned and ran. Ned's leg was nearly severed and had to be amputated. The shooter got away, unidentified. Things eventually settled down again after this latest outrage, the worst yet, although everyone knew that the culprit was still out there.

In due course came my junior year at Southern Huntingdon County High School. I was kept busy maintaining my grades in the Home Economics curriculum. I'd switched from the business classes, considering my prospects. Thanks to a program whose details I don't remember now, I was accepted into the Empire Beauty School in Lewistown and was due to start classes there around May 20 – two days a week plus Saturdays.

There I was at seventeen, doing my best to make something of myself. My parents had done well with eighth-grade educations. I'd graduate, learn a trade, and move away to pursue a career and a family of my own. I looked forward to more than raising my kids in a series of rundown rentals in the same places where I grew up. I wanted, not so much to be rich, as to have some nice things around me that weren't invariably hand-me-downs. To achieve any of this I knew I'd have to be well-presented, as well as hard-working. I'd learned to use makeup by the time I was in high school, thanks to an aunt with Avon samples. According to the fashion of the times, I wore eyebrow pencil and lipstick and a small dab of rouge, even at home in the evenings.

Thanksgiving, deer season, and Christmas came and went that year, with us harvesting turkeyfoot trailing pine and twining it over coat-hanger wire for wreaths to sell. Winter came in earnest, and went. Spring and Easter came early, the evenings grew longer and the rain came and stayed, and we gathered wildflowers for Mom; smelly as it was, blooming mountain laurel was a favorite. Finally, the end of the school year was in sight. Our bus driver Mr. Frehn, as always, warned us to keep our hands inside the windows or Bad Things Would Happen, with the growing branches scraping the sides of the school bus as it wound along the narrow roads.

Wednesday, the eleventh of May, was a big day for me. The high school's very first student fashion show was that evening. I'd spent a great deal of time and effort in Home Economics class on the suit I was going to model. It was light blue, almost lavender, and fully lined in a slippery satiny fabric that had given me fits, trying to get the lining to ride right in the sleeves of the jacket. Mom could help me with practically every other domestic skill, but I was on my own when it came to sewing. Mrs. Keith, my teacher, was to pick me up and bring me back that evening, otherwise I couldn't have attended the event.

As we always did when going straight home from school, all six of us got off the bus at the end of our lane on that beautiful, balmy Wednesday afternoon in May, and began the walk back to our house.

Chapter 2

Our bus stop was where our road intersected Pleasant Hill Road, right across from the old Dick Miller farm. It was about half a mile back to our house – far enough that we'd crowd into the car in cold weather and be driven to and from the bus.

But not that day: Wednesday, May 11, 1966.

My teacher was to pick me up that evening to take me to the fashion show. That left me an hour and a half in which to greet my little dog Tiny at the door, do homework and chores, eat supper, and get cleaned up and ready.

After a lot of rain over the previous week, the weather had turned nice that afternoon. We were just about out of sight of Pleasant Hill Road, long before we could see our house down the lane, when it happened. My brothers were walking ahead and my three younger sisters were crowded around me, watching for deer.

Nothing appeared to be out of the ordinary until a man stood up from behind a tree and stepped onto the road between us and Jim.

The man wore drab clothes, as if hunting, and his head was bowed under an orange baseball cap. When he looked up, we could see that he hid his eyes under thick, old-fashioned green motorcycle goggles – but the first thing that we saw was the sawed-off shotgun he leveled at us.

For a fraction of a second we froze, uncomprehending.

Then he pointed the shotgun at each child in turn. "I don't want any bullsh-t out of any of you." He passed over my younger siblings. "You're too young." Then he got to me. "You're what I'm looking for. You can keep up."

I dropped my tablet and chemistry book and black sweater; instinctively I went for them, but he grabbed me by the back of the neck in a grip so strong that it hurt.

"Leave that! You'll never need it again," he

ordered.

I managed to gasp out to my family to *go*, that I'd be all right. The man dragged me off the road into the brush, down across the stream, then up the low ridge beyond. When we reached the top, he made me stop and sit.

I could hear my father calling my name. For the first time I could ever remember, I disobeyed him. I didn't answer. I had a knife at my neck and the muzzle of a gun in my mouth.

"Forget him," the kidnapper commanded. "You'll never hear that voice again. Forget all of them. You're mine now."

Trying to grasp what was going on, I was only able to pray: *oh my God, there are more of them and they're going to slaughter my family.* Until I heard Dad calling, I thought that this man might already have been to our house and killed him.

Then the calling stopped, and we were running again, down the far side of the low ridge, across the stream in the next hollow and up the other side – then retracing our steps back downhill, into the water, to follow the swollen current downstream. Much later I learned that this was where a bloodhound would lose our scent, as the kidnapper planned.

He drove me across country, through thick woods, skirting open fields and the power line right-of-way, the brush whipping welts into my legs. Then it was back into water – this time, to cross Decorum Road where runoff from Mushroom Hollow (where we went to pick mushrooms) flooded over the pavement. The kidnapper simply ordered me across the road, apparently without caring that a car might come.

Once in Mushroom Hollow, we stopped by the stream flowing down from the mountain. "I'm going to show you how to drink," declared the man. "Get *down!*"

He kicked my legs out from under me, grabbing my hair and dunking my head under the water three or four times, then hauling me to my feet, still by the hair. Gasping for breath and half-blinded by water, I was dragged up Neelyton Mountain.

Somewhere along the way, he pulled a chain out from his shoulder bag or a pocket. It must have been weighing him down; it was a big, rusty logging chain, and it had a padlock. It went around my neck and didn't come off for nearly a week. Then he tied my hands together with rope, making it even more difficult to keep my balance as he forced me through the dense underbrush.

There's a point about halfway up these mountain ridges where the merely steep and rocky slope becomes practically vertical, and at this point there is a natural game trail along the mountainside. Our course changed, and we ran south along the ridge down that trail.

I say *ran*, and run we did, but our progress wasn't straightforward. It can't be in these woods. I soon learned that this man would stop dead to listen for a few seconds, and I wasn't to move a muscle or make the slightest sound or he'd threaten to shoot me. Then he'd make me run again.

"We're going to the Golden Egg," he said once, when we had paused on the trail. He grabbed my cheeks, hard, and yelled right in my face. "The *Golden Egg!* Do you understand what I'm telling you, bitch?" He spat in my face. "You know how to drive, right? You'd better know how to f – in' drive. You'll drive or I'll f – in' blow your damn head off!"

I'd never driven on an actual hard road before or at any great speed, but I realized that I'd better believe I could figure out enough to stay alive if the time came. I had no idea what exactly he had in mind, though, until we were nearing the Tuscarora Tunnel.

"The Golden Egg," he said, looking at the Turnpike. "That's the Golden Egg. We're gonna get on there and you're gonna drive me to Mifflintown." It made no sense to me, then or now, because the Turnpike doesn't go anywhere near Mifflintown, but I wasn't about to point that out to him. It would only get me killed.

We had covered some distance, and it was dark by the time we descended to a hard road again. We passed under the Turnpike on Locke Road, then moved back up into the woods. This time we paralleled the course of Locke Road, which ends at the Fannettsburg Road as that road ascends the mountain. We crossed there and slid down into another stream, followed that down the mountain, waded through the swamp it flowed into, and crossed another road – this time the Cowans Gap road.

We were approaching the Turnpike again right outside Burnt Cabins. Instead of crossing back under the highway into the village, or finding a place to hide for the night, the gunman had me begin to climb in the dark.

It was nearing dawn by the time we reached

his goal: no less than the very summit of Sidney's Knob. It's the highest point at that end of the valley, with a magnificent view that extends for miles. I'd never been there, of course. How far had we come? I was too terrified to think of such a detail, unable to think of anything but staying alive for the next moments.

The kidnapper, on the other hand, was celebrating. I had to watch as he stomped and danced about, hollering gibberish that sounded as if he were speaking in tongues, as he watched the lights drive by on the Turnpike below.

I couldn't dwell on it at the time, but that sight was beautiful: white lights one way, red the other, on the pale concrete.

He tired of the amusement soon enough. As the sky began to lighten with the dawn, he looked down at the valley below him, and at the Turnpike, and I distinctly heard his words.

"I'll see you again."

It began to rain again that day.

He had us retrace our steps to the base of the knob, then sent me into the stream that flowed through a culvert under the Turnpike and past the old gristmill, then detoured around Burnt Cabins. We went under Route 522 via another bridge, up a hollow, and eventually climbed up the side of Shade Mountain on the west side of the valley.

For the rest of Thursday, he took us north until we were nearly above Shade Gap, but he began to re-cross the valley just south of the town, behind the picnic grounds. From there it was down to another stream, wading along it and getting out only when we were almost within sight of Route 641, the Neelyton road.

By this time, it was dark again. We worked our way through the woods near the road. I knew we were passing near the houses of both Uncle Guy and Ned Price, but there was never a chance to get away, bound as I was; nor did I have any means to contact anyone, with this man watching my every move, his shotgun always trained at my back. We came near Neelyton, went south of the village and south of the barn and farmyard at the foot of Neelyton Mountain, and once again began to climb.

Friday's false dawn found us at the top of Neelyton Mountain, near a dump not far from the road. We kept on. As we angled down, a tawny form crouching on a rock slab caught my eye. Mountain lions are supposed to be extinct here, but I have the proof of my own eyes that says otherwise. This one was interested in us, staring as if it were sizing up meat on the hoof. "Too far away for a shot," grunted the kidnapper, distracting me. When I looked back, the lion had gone. The last I saw of it was a glimpse as it went down the slope, in the same direction we were going.

I was terrified enough already without the fear that it might lie in wait for us down there.

He took us south again, along the same route we had used Wednesday night. Before we descended to Locke Road and its underpass, he looked at the Turnpike, long and hard, busy with Friday's steady traffic going to and from the Tuscarora Mountain tunnel, and something about that normal activity angered him.

We climbed Sidney's Knob again.

Right at the top of the peak was a hole, almost a cave: a loose slab fallen over a gap in the bedrock, some three or four feet deep and not quite high enough to stand in. He reached inside and pulled out a corroded can, opening it by stabbing the rusty blade of a hunting knife into the lid and working it around, heedless of the jagged edges. He said he'd show me how to eat, then tipped it up above his face and wolfed down as much of the spilling contents as he could catch in his gaping mouth – peas.

After he was done, he "fed" me. I don't know where he learned how polite society ate their peas a generation or more before, but he picked three dirty peas off the ground, placed them precisely in a row on the blade of his knife and then grabbed my jaw, squeezing until I opened my mouth. Somehow, he didn't spill the peas or slice the back of my throat when he put the blade into my mouth, so far back that the sharp point gagged me.

"Do you feel that?" he asked, and spat in my face. "Do you feel it?" Then he twisted it sideways for the peas to roll off.

"That's all you're getting," he said, then he added: "Ever."

That day seemed to have been the man's original goal. By then, he'd apparently expected any search for me to have been abandoned, and he'd thought he could take me onto the Turnpike and flag down a car on its own to hijack, without any other motorists noticing. Then, he kept saying, we'd go to Mifflintown.

But things weren't working out according to his plans. Turnpike traffic had been just as heavy as usual on Friday morning, and the search that had begun with Dad shouting after me had expanded, not fizzled out. There were too many people intruding into his domain.

We started the entire circuit over again, still in the intermittent rain. He didn't like rain; it made too much noise and impeded his vision, and silenced other people's sounds. He didn't like noise, or lights, or people that might see him, and now there was too much going on. He seemed to expect the whole valley to abide by the same rhythm and routine as always, never thinking that what he'd done would spark much of a response.

I honestly don't think he expected anyone but Dad to make more than a cursory search for me, and now there were cars and trucks, helicopters and small planes, and people where they shouldn't be – distractions at all hours. Disruptions to how he envisioned his plan unfolding. People butting into his business.

As we went, he held the chain and the shotgun in his right hand. In his left was a little portable radio, held close to his ear. I never heard what he listened to, but he kept up a muttered monologue about "the dumb bastards" and every now and again he might alter our course after listening intently for a while.

By Friday night, he was circling us around just south of Shade Gap once more. There was a lot of activity at Harper Memorial Park, where the Shade Gap Picnic is still held. The kidnapper had us go around the back end of the park so that he could get a look at what was going on.

We were passing within shouting distance of the headquarters of a massive manhunt, and we were not seen or heard by a single soul.

Chapter 3

I can put bare facts down, like where we went and what happened, but they can't convey what it was like in the company of this man.

He wore layer upon layer of clothes, all of them reeking. He had no whole teeth, just black stubs, and his breath was as foul as his language.

There was nothing of compassion about him – no consideration for me or anyone else, or anything else for that matter. There was only anger and rage, which he took out on me because I was within reach and couldn't fight back. Practically every time he opened his mouth it was to scream that he'd kill something or someone or me.

And he'd spit. Where that came from, I can't even guess. When he shouted at me – he seldom just *spoke* – he'd grab my cheeks, hard, as if he would rip the skin right off. Then he'd spit in my face.

He mostly had two ways of speaking: a low mutter for himself, and an angry, excited scream for me or anything else that displeased him. When he did talk or grunt, it was often to someone or something I couldn't see, but he never explained himself to me. I never knew exactly whom he thought he was addressing, be it leaves, or air, or other people only he sensed.

Everything he did focused on *control:* of me, and of all the world around him. As far as I was concerned, that control went far beyond the bonds around my neck and my wrists.

"Look at me. I'm ugly, ain't I?" he taunted me. When I twitched an eyeball to comply, he responded with instantaneous anger. *"DON'T YOU LOOK AT ME, BITCH! I'm the ugliest sonofabitch you've ever seen! Don't you look at me!"*

In the rage that followed my legs were kicked out from under me so that I fell and slid down the slope. That was only another excuse to accuse me of attempting to escape. I was pulled to my feet by the chain and by my hair, and once more I had to run through the woods he knew so well.

The valley was his world, and he thought of it that way. Everything, down to the trees and the wind, had better do as he said or he'd shoot them. When he fired, he never aimed; he just pointed the shotgun or the pistol, and mostly hit whatever he pointed at. He'd obviously never been taught how to shoot properly. He'd pop off at anything with that sawed-off shotgun: deer or other game, waving branches, or whatever. He did it just for the fun of seeing something run or shatter, without a thought for the racket or the ammunition he ran through.

He hated noise unless he was the one making it, and these woods are never silent. Nighttime in the mountains, when the animals come out and the trees creak and rustle, is as noisy as in a town, if not more so.

The only name he would call me by, aside from "bitch," was "Blue Eyes." I was a mannequin to be threatened and intimidated and beaten until I ceased to display any human reactions. I was to be run around the mountains bound by that chain until people stopped caring about me, and I stopped caring about anything at all except whatever he wanted. Then I was to drive him in a stolen car wherever he wanted to go.

"You're going to be exactly what I want you to be," he told me from the first day, spitting on me, then shoving the palm of his hand in my face and smearing the spit around. "Aren't you, bitch? *AREN'T YOU?*"

As we went, there might be a few minutes of near-peace, now and again. Then would come a yank on my hair or on the chain, a blow to the body or face, a screaming rant or a real beating, just to remind me that I was under his control. He never let go of the chain, so when he struck with that hand, it was followed by a blow to my side from the heavy links.

Every time I stumbled or fell, I was "trying to get away," and he'd pull me back onto my feet by my hair. Every day he'd say it was a good day to kill me, "but maybe I won't bother." "Maybe" was never a thing I could count on. There were too many times when his constant irritation at my presence escalated, and he would try to work himself into a killing rage. Had he ever done so, the only thing that could have spared my life would have been if the kidnapper couldn't decide whether to blast me with the shotgun, or to use the knife or his bare hands.

There was no real sleep; he never slept for more than a minute or two, and we never stopped for longer than maybe ten minutes, and very seldom that. When we did stop, it was only where there was cover. Under mountain laurel bushes was a favorite, especially when it rained, with the dense leaves acting as an umbrella. Dark stands of stunted, jagged jack pines were another favorite.

I was forced through all the kinds of brush and all the different footings there are on those mountains and in that valley. Pitch dark or daylight made no difference; the kidnapper was never lost. I couldn't match his skill, and I got yelled at and hit for not being able to cross the steep rockslides of loose sandstone slabs without having them shift and grind under me.

He would always drive me straight ahead through whatever growth was in the way, stopping in places he seemed to find familiar, resting where there was cover and a view. But after five minutes or so, the place would be "no good" – he'd think there were men closing in on him, and we'd be off again.

Anytime we stopped, he wound the loose

end of the chain around a tree and padlocked it. He would sit close with the shotgun or revolver handy, as well as a knife.

He loved to torment me with the knife. "Maybe I'll cut off your nose. Or your eyes. Or just your throat," he would say as he drew the knife over my face. "I'll cut off your hair when we get where we're going and everyone will think you're a boy. No one will know you." He'd slip the blade up past my hairline. "Whoops!" Or he'd stick the pistol in my face. "Blue Eyes all over the place. Poof."

When he saw that he'd frightened me, he'd giggle and laugh and dance around.

As I sat, if I dropped off to sleep or if I shifted in the slightest, I was "trying to pull something" – trying to escape – and the abuse and the running would start again.

As I was dragged up Neelyton Mountain again in the night, I was "watered" once more, having my legs kicked out from under me and my head dunked by the hair in runoff flowing down from the mountain. There had been those three peas and, true to the kidnapper's word, nothing more. The weight dropping from me was no longer just water.

I had stepped off the school bus on Wednesday afternoon in a white shirt and a simple red corduroy dress, the sort we called a shift, with a black sweater and my class ring. My school shoes had been open sandals, light-colored with a black bow. They were cheap things from the five-and-dime store, the soles mended with tire glue to last until the end of school. They were hardly suited for a day on my feet at a job or out shopping, and certainly unsuitable for hiking over some sixty or seventy miles of rough terrain.

The sweater had been dropped with my school things when I'd been taken. The shoes had left pieces all along the path I'd been forced to tread – and so had my feet. Tough though they were, they were cut to ribbons within a few days, the skin blistered and entirely gone in places. Whatever state I was in, though, I felt no pain that I ever remembered.

And so it went until Saturday. I'm fairly certain it was Saturday, anyway.

On that morning, something changed. There was yet another beating; eventually I realized that the radio was gone, or at least he'd put it away because it was dead, and it was somehow my fault. How the batteries had lasted as long as they had anyway, I can't fathom.

That morning was when the kidnapper took off his outer jacket, pants, and rubber boots, and threw them at me. That left him with some two or three layers still on him, I guessed, and a pair of ordinary hunting boots that had been under the black galoshes all this time.

"You're red. They can see you. Put those on so's you look human," he ordered, poking the shotgun into my gut. "You're ugly. That red dress sticks out like a sore thumb. You shouldn't look like a girl, you'll just get me killed. You should look like a boy."

I put the things on over my own clothes, the shotgun at my head, then his hand slapping me when I didn't move quickly enough. I doubt he ever laundered any of his clothes, and he had never stopped for hygiene of any sort. I had been in the second day of my period when I was abducted, but by now I was too dehydrated for that to matter.

I still can't stand the scent of unwashed human.

He threw some baling twine at me and I tied the boots on tightly. They might have had newspaper or rags stuffed in the bottom; I've never been sure, and my feet couldn't feel anything by that point.

The jacket had a sort of vest lining in it, and a lump in the side pocket. "There's a hat in the pocket. Put it on," he commanded. I did so; my hair, filthy and matted after the past days, was long enough to hang down my neck, but was now hidden inside the jacket and under the hat.

"Now you look like me," he said. "They'll shoot you first." It was true. He was only two or three inches taller than I was, no more, and I'm short.

From then on, I was sent out in front to draw fire as well as to stay under his eye.

All along, he'd been demanding that I tell him who he was, insisting that I knew him. That came to a head later that day. He removed an odd device from his mouth, two wooden discs strung together with wire, and his cheeks fell in, making him look older.

"You know who I am," he spat. "Say it!"

"I'm sorry! I don't know who you are!" I answered again as I had before, bracing myself, knowing he'd start hitting me when he grew frustrated enough.

"Never saw me in Murphy's store? I saw

you there all the time with your daddy. I know who your daddy is. Short, bald sonofabitch."

I still couldn't remember him. He slapped my face. "Say my name!" Again, harder. "Say it, you dumb bitch!" Over and over. Then he started in with his fists.

Blood ran from my broken nose before it finally it burst out of him. "I'm Bicycle Pete! The one you make fun of in the school bus!"

I knew who Bicycle Pete was. I'd seen him from the bus, of course, and one night Darlene Mentzer and I had been on our way home from Chambersburg by way of Cowan's Gap when a movement in the headlights caught her eye.

"What's he doing here?" she'd asked rhetorically. The hunched-over figure had been pushing a bicycle along the berm, a flashlight in its front basket. She hadn't offered him a ride.

People would see him all over, from Chambersburg to Mount Union and beyond, riding or pushing that bike, often with a little dog in the basket.

"And now you know," continued Bicycle Pete. "I'll have to kill you when I'm done."

That day he began to brag more, too. It was nothing but another way of impressing me, intimidating me, controlling me.

Things began to fall into place. I didn't dare show it, of course, but the effect on me was different than he anticipated. I was learning about this kidnapper, but not necessarily just what he wanted me to know.

"I tried that old bitch, but she was so damned f – in' dumb. Too old an' dumb." I connected that with Mrs. Jacka, a tough older lady who lived in one of the houses across the covered bridge from St. Mary's church. Somehow, though, I think she impressed him; she'd been alone at home, but she'd taken action and escaped. She lived very much as he did, in fact – she walked from Shade Gap to Rockhill every day, using the railroad tracks and carrying a long, heavy flashlight. Then she worked eight or nine hours on her feet at the American Legion, and walked the miles back home unless someone offered her a ride to her run-down house. I think, too, that she was his first real attempt, a test that had proven more challenging than expected.

The lady who had been stopped by the logs across the road was Mrs. Yohn, and he called her "just a dumb bitch." He never mentioned her baby as such, only that "some damned thing was yellin' and screamin'. The damn noise was some damn f – in' kid, I think." The noise would have simply enraged this man, and made him react as indeed he had – by shooting up the car.

Children were nobodies to him, just *things* that screamed. "I suppose you heard about that kid up the road in Tyrone. Wasn't me. I don't mess with damned kids." That would have been Kathy Shea. The distance would have been nothing to him, I knew that by then, but there was no cause for him to go there and no one saw him there that day, and I never saw any reason to doubt him. Bicycle Pete would not have gone into an unfamiliar town crowded with people to take a useless child with only his bicycle. Many years later, other things are coming out about that case, none of them relevant to my kidnapping. It does stand out, however, as the only comment I remember from Bicycle Pete that explained an unrelated matter.

A long, long time later, I was able to pass that bit of unintended reassurance along to her family.

However, he boasted readily of Ned and Jessie Price. "I'd'a taken that f – in' bitch but *he* came out, and I just had to shoot him." Mrs. Price hadn't even been at home; had he known that? He'd probably have waited and abducted her, with the car, as she pulled in to her driveway.

"I get what I want," he continued. "I chose you. I'll kill anyone that gets in my way. I'd'a had you at your uncle's but you went down and shot off your big mouth." I remembered that summer night, two years before, when a man had tried to get in through the upstairs window at my uncle's house, into my room. Uncle Guy had thought it was a drunk from the bar down the road.

What I really expected him to brag about was the woman who had grabbed a rifle when a masked intruder broke in through her back door, only to have it shot out of her hand. I've heard several versions over the years – from the intruder bandaging her hand and leaving, to taking her outside to rape her, successfully or not.

Had it really been this man who attacked her, however, he would have found it hilarious to shoot a gun out of a woman's hand, and would not have been able to keep from gloating about it. And, rather than being raped and allowed to go home, the woman would have been kidnapped as I was, or killed, and her gun would surely have been taken even if it was damaged.

This man had never yet displayed to me any inclination whatsoever for sex, and toward me he never would. Instead, he was fascinated with blood, and pain, and violence, with possession and control. Instead of sex, Bicycle Pete was after something entirely different.

"We're getting up on that Turnpike," he'd told me ever since the evening he kidnapped me. "We're getting up there. I'm going to shoot someone and get their car. And you'd better know how to drive, you f – in' bitch, or I'll just get one of *them* to drive and I'll shoot your f – in' head off."

Mrs. Yohn had been driving a car. Jessie Price would have returned home in Ned's. Uncle Guy's had been parked at his place. I knew now that this man had been watching me for years. My sisters and I would borrow old blankets and make a playhouse out in the woods; but it was in a place a car could get to. I didn't have my license, but I could drive our station wagon around the lanes by our house.

I was never under any illusions. He may have chosen me, a girl old enough to drive but smaller than he was, because he felt that a girl wouldn't fight back like a boy could. He'd chosen a pretty girl, so that he had one more thing he could control and take away from me at his whim with hands or knife. He'd kill anyone that got in the way – and me, when he decided that he wasn't happy with me. Then he'd go on to the next girl who could drive.

Other things had begun to happen by Saturday, too. Not only was I losing weight and dressed like Bicycle Pete, but thoughts were careening around in my head after days without food or water or rest.

Most important to me were thoughts of my family. Were they even still alive, or had they been murdered? Was all this happening because Bicycle Pete suddenly had accomplices? Had there been a prison break? Was there a gang on the loose? Had they gotten at my family?

According to the kidnapper, I would never know. I couldn't ask, of course; I wasn't to speak unless he demanded a response. I was to forget everything I'd ever known. I had no family. There wasn't to be any *me;* there should only be him and his will. Anything else, any indication of a reaction, any independence on my part, would see me dead and left on the trail while he went off after someone else.

But amidst all the noise both inside and

outside my head, cutting through everything on which I had to focus just to survive in the kidnapper's presence, a persistent voice clamored for my attention, inexplicably telling me that I would not only survive, but that I'd be all right. I wasn't sure what to make of it. All I knew was that it meant that I must soon face a choice – maybe my last choice between death and life. Death would be so easy to provoke now, so much easier than the effort it took to stay alive.

And I was so tired.

Chapter 4

Something else came into play over that weekend: time and memory began to run together for me. I have tried to keep events in order, but some things have been my best guesses after fifty years of recollections that were haphazard even at the time.

For instance, when I was taken on Wednesday the kidnapper had worn a canvas bag slung across his shoulder. I remember that it would entangle his shotgun, and that he had finally thrown it away in a rage. But for decades I didn't remember exactly where or when. I only knew it was found later.

Exactly which time of the three times that I

was taken up Sidney's Knob I was fed three peas, I can't recall, except that it wasn't the very first trip. And for many years, I was more confused than I ever realized about what happened with Bicycle Pete's dogs.

One thing I am sure of is that we visited his home once, and once only. From other events, and from the fact that I was dressed in his clothes by then, I'm going to say it was no later than Saturday evening. It was around sundown, which was about eight P.M. that week. We had bypassed Burnt Cabins once more. The courses he'd taken around the valley so far mostly used the same trails while moving north and south on the mountains themselves, but varied and zigzagged when we crossed the valley so that we didn't often repeat movements anywhere near people.

This evening we went up yet another hollow to skirt and then to cross a field, and approach a shack. There were several right by 522; I'd seen them before from the highway but never paid any attention. The largest one had a chimney. Now, I could hear dogs barking inside.

Something bothered him about the door – he knew someone had been there prying, pawing at *his* property, and he was angry about it – but still he opened it with one hand while he held me against the doorframe by my throat with the other. The door opened inwards. He pushed me with it as a decoy and edged his revolver inside, but there was no one there except three dogs. Still one-handed, he managed to grab a bag of dog food – I heard the pellets spill on the floor – but then two of the dogs ran out. A large one and a small, yappy one bounded out past me, happily playing. They wouldn't go back inside, and he couldn't catch them while controlling me, so they stayed out. He shut the door on the last dog and kicked it the rest of the way in, locked the cabin, and we were off again, back through the field. We hadn't been there five minutes, and I never got a good look around inside.

When we reached the treeline, I realized that we weren't alone. The yappy little dog was following us. The man snapped at it to go home, but it didn't.

He raised the shotgun. "F – ing stupid dog," he said, and pulled the trigger at least once. I didn't see what happened, I just heard a yelp, and then we were off again. I had no way of knowing if the dog was dead or if it had run away, but for years I was sure it had been killed.

Just before he took us into the woods,

something caught my eye, a movement back at the cabin. Was that a man I saw, running away from the building? It was no more than a glimpse, and of course I said nothing.

Afterward, he took us west to Shade Mountain again, and back around the valley. Sometime during these days and nights, we went by Burnt Cabins in the dark. I remember seeing searchers, and I thought that if Dad were there he'd have had something to say to them. One man shone a flashlight around. I could almost have reached out and touched another who was lighting up a cigarette: destroying his night vision, making a smell and a light to pinpoint himself by, when he knew there might be an armed enemy out there. But I still had the shotgun trained on me as I half-waded, half-swam through a neck-deep hole in a narrow stream, and could not give myself away.

If my condition was deteriorating, so was the kidnapper's. Early on I had realized that he had moods that swung far beyond my experience. For many years I didn't say much about it, but when I did, I found that I hadn't been mistaken.

Bicycle Pete had different personalities. I remember his eyes as a sort of grayish hazel that changed with his moods, which were getting more violent and erratic the longer I was with him, from red rage that almost literally choked him to glimpses of a desperate fear. At the time, I believed him to be possessed. Even after knowing more about dissociated identities, I still believe he was possessed, and as thoroughly evil as a human could be.

That isn't to say that I truly hated him then, or hate him now; not with the loathing that he felt toward me. Of course, I could not *like* him, or the situation he put me in, in any sense of the word; but it didn't take long for me to work out that no one can just grow up to be the way he was. Even before I knew anything else about him, I knew that he was ill, and that he wasn't wholly responsible for what he did.

I realized that that was the choice I faced: I had to decide who *I* was, and what kind of person and what kind of Christian I would be for the rest of my life, however short that might be. At seventeen, I could begin to recognize that real hatred – no matter how justified by what this man did to myself and others – would hurt me far worse than anything he could do to me.

All along, I heard the voice that stayed with me. I seemed to hear someone saying that I was doing well, that I'd be all right. Did I dare believe that? It flew in the face of the evidence, as far as I was concerned, but of course I wanted to believe that I'd survive this. I just didn't see how I could.

Despair hammered at me all the while, too. How long could I keep up, how could I keep on taking every blow he inflicted on me? How long before he shot me or cut my throat? He kept saying that I'd never see my family again, telling me to forget them, that they were gone. Were they even still alive? Had there been others to murder them?

If they were dead, I didn't want to go home.

It's an uncomfortable fact, but what kept me alive during my time with the kidnapper was what I'd learned from watching Mom. I responded as if this man were a violent drunk, like Dad could be after a weekend binge, and I credit that with saving my life. I hadn't been in Bicycle Pete's company a day before I realized that there would never be any communication between us, and probably never again between him and any other human. I never addressed him; the only way to stay alive was to take his abuse, physical, verbal, and mental, and keep on.

Day and night, light and dark, logging road

and thick underbrush spun around me. How did this man keep going, and how long would he go without rest or food? Once more that I remember, he let me drink, this time shoving me backward as I waded and holding me under as if I were being drowned, or baptized.

Once, I managed to sneak a birch twig, and was able to chew for a few minutes before he noticed and ripped it out of my mouth. As he did I clamped my teeth hard enough to strip the bark and the shredded end off, and thankfully he didn't see that I had something left to chew on as he sent me ahead of him. I worked that wad of bark and wood fiber around as long as I could. The longer I did, the softer it became and the sweeter it tasted. It got my mouth wet, it cleaned my teeth, and when the taste finally subsided I swallowed it. It was no bigger than a piece of used-up gum by then and, like those few peas days ago, couldn't count as a meal – but I had done something for myself. It was a victory, and it tasted heavenly.

The next time I could spare the attention to take in my surroundings was Sunday evening, I think. I knew the immediate area; it wasn't far from a place we'd rented some years before. We'd waded along a creek, which was nothing new, but at that point we had entered a swamp where Mountain Foot Road zigzags around a farm. Being downhill from a farm with cattle made the stench of the mud that much worse.

Here he stopped. I didn't dare ask why, but I could see that he was watching the farmhouse. I have no idea how long he had us stay there, but it was just before sundown when a car pulled away from the place. When it was out of sight, he moved.

He never hesitated. He went up to the back door, broke the glass, reached in, and turned the doorknob. Then it was through the kitchen and straight upstairs. As always, I was in front with the shotgun held on me, so I didn't see him pick up anything in the kitchen.

When we reached a bedroom, he pushed me onto the bed and held me there with the shotgun in one hand while he opened a dresser drawer with the other. He rifled through the top drawer – I think it was socks and underwear – and didn't find what he was looking for, so he moved to the next one down.

Ever since, I've felt sure that he had been in that house before. It's a creepy thought that he might have enjoyed hiding inside while the elderly owners went about their day, but I can see him doing just that – because in the second drawer he found exactly what he wanted. He pulled out a little semiautomatic pistol.

Immediately I was shoved out of the room, nearly falling down the stairs, and then it was out the front door and away up toward Shade Mountain. Once again, we couldn't have been in there five minutes, and he had accomplished what he set out to do.

He was over the moon, like a kid at Christmas with the toy he'd wanted forever. He never showed as much elation over kidnapping a person as he did over getting that gun. In his triumph, he was generous: he offered me an apple he must have snatched up as he sent me ahead through the kitchen.

I couldn't take it. I was starving, I needed that food, but I was too sick to accept it. It wasn't mine. I'd just been through a house that wasn't mine. Up until this point, I hadn't participated in any wrongdoing beyond trespassing, and I was too upset to begin now. My parents had never, ever tolerated thieving.

I refused it, and took the consequences. He threw the thing on the ground before he hit me. I don't know what became of another apple I saw that he had taken for himself, but I never saw him eat it, although of course I had my back to him most of the time.

As we headed back toward Shade Gap, I remember looking back at the house, seeing it sink into the dark evening mist that rose as the sun went down behind the mountain.

I'm not sure how close to the town we were when we crossed the valley. Dawn on Monday saw us back on Neelyton Mountain, near where we'd first climbed up all those days ago. We spooked some deer, and started seeing people in the distance, so this time he took us over to Shade Mountain without going as far south as we had before.

His orbit seemed to be shrinking, drawing in toward his home and whatever precious possessions bound him to his cabin.

Chapter 5

It was on Monday, I'm fairly certain, that I really noticed another change. Not only was Bicycle Pete's foul temper even more unpredictable, but so were our movements. In part, it might have been because he had a project in mind.

Today he sent us up Gobbler's Knob, heading south rather than circling north again. At one point, we were almost in open terrain when we heard a helicopter. Bicycle Pete ordered me to wrap my arms around a tree. The helicopter passed over without spotting us.

Sometime late in the day we were atop a steep bank, almost a cliff, above a branch of the

Little Aughwick creek. A tree had fallen, pulling up the earth with its roots, and in the depression thus formed was a square lard can, barely hidden under leaves and branches.

"Get that out," he ordered. "Open it! Can't you do anything right, bitch?"

I dragged it out, then wrestled it open. Inside was some sort of paper. Whether it was printed or written on I wasn't sure, but it was not blank. He took one of his pistols – I couldn't tell which – and slammed it into the can, cursing. "Bury that!"

I scooped the hole a little deeper with my hands, took the can and put it back in. Instead of waiting while I shoved dirt on it, he just kicked debris over the top and got us out of there.

After that, we continued south along the stream, at least for a while; but he seemed to have lost his focus. We turned and went back the way we came, and kept going north through the dark.

Perhaps it was Monday that another thing happened that I remember. He took us to another of his hideaways, another void in the bedrock, covered by a wooden door with rocks cemented to it. He looked inside, but immediately he grunted and closed it up again. I didn't get a good look, but from the way he acted I thought it held nothing he wanted just then. As quickly as he could, he sent us away from there, as if something had spooked him.

In any case, we didn't go as far as Shade Gap, nor do I remember going across the valley to Neelyton Mountain, although we kept moving all night. Instead we simply turned again and went back the way we came.

It wasn't lost on me that we were staying near his shack. He was possessive and greedy, incessantly fretting about his belongings, but he must have been leery of going back there without the radio to keep him informed of the movements of the manhunt.

The next morning found us in a jack pine thicket somewhere to the east of Mountain Foot Road, not too far from his cabin. Bicycle Pete had me sit with my back to a pine trunk, chained to it by the neck as usual. He sat with his hand on the shotgun and his back to another tree. Before us was a clearing along a logging road, last year's tall yellowed grass thick above the greener mat of this spring's growth, the open area ringed around with dense brush. Beyond the pines, the bushes and hardwoods were beginning to come into leaf.

It might be that we followed the same

pattern I'd had to get used to over the past days, and perhaps we drowsed for two or three minutes – or, just maybe, longer and more soundly. The sun was warm. I had been facing a bright, empty clearing. Then I blinked, and a man had appeared.

Because of the tall grass and weeds I could only see him from the waist up through the pine branches, but he wasn't well-dressed for the woods. I glanced toward Bicycle Pete.

I had no hope at all of stopping what happened next, even if there had been a chance. The blasts rang in my ears, the man stopped in his tracks, and there was a sudden confusion as dogs came at us from left and right – huge German Shepherds, heads and teeth filling my vision as I sat defenseless on the ground and tried to shield myself. More shots at the dogs, then the chain went slack and I was made to run, away from the man I was sure had been killed, away from the racket and noise I couldn't understand.

I was absolutely certain that I would be the next to be shot.

When we finally stopped, I was in shock, stunned and appalled, but Bicycle Pete was shouting that he'd killed that sonofabitch and his dogs. The celebration that followed was ghastly.

He danced, stomping and whooping like a child playing at a war dance, completely possessed in his elation. He'd killed a man. He was on top of his world, invincible and unconquerable.

But soon enough, anger took over. I hadn't joined in the celebrating. Why? Was I too dumb to know how he'd saved me, killing that man and those dogs? I should be happy. I should know he was the cleverest, strongest, most powerful man on earth. I was ungrateful, that's what I was.

He started beating me. He grabbed my hair, hit my face, kicked me in the stomach, and kept on punching me.

And where had the padlock gone, and the chain? He'd been carrying them after he'd unchained me, but they were somehow gone and it was my fault. What was I trying to pull? Did I think I could get away?

The rage and the blows went on. It was the worst beating he'd ever given me.

I was too numb to feel it. If I wanted to live at all, I couldn't; I dared not feel a thing.

All I could see was that man in the clearing, whole one instant, dying the next.

When it was done, and the rage was spent for the moment, the paranoia came to the fore once again.

"This place is no good," he grunted. "They can see me. Move, bitch."

For me, things changed a little after that. I was too much trouble. He hated me. He ought to just shoot me. He'd always said that; but now, despite having killed a man and being the most powerful creature in his world, his plans were going sour. Obviously, it was all my fault. I was the whole problem.

Up until now, it had been hard enough to keep a step ahead of him mentally; now, it became even harder. His moods swung more violently than ever, the separate personalities more clear and distinct, but not a one of them with any trace of compassion or humanity.

He'd sent us down a logging road through a hollow away from the site of the shooting, over a low ridge to Mountain Foot Road and across that, and into Potts Gap. At that point he changed his mind and we doubled back, starting up Gobbler's Knob by way of a particularly steep and difficult ridge.

As we went, we had to cross a rockslide. Just as we'd gotten back onto firm ground, there was the rumble and clatter of the great slabs shifting, grinding downhill in a brief avalanche until they settled again.

The kidnapper grunted, barely looking around. "Only a second, and I wouldn't be bothered with you anymore, bitch."

Not far away, where I couldn't see and wouldn't know about for some time, other things were changing. A man had been killed – not just any man, but an FBI agent. As we'd crossed Mountain Foot Road afterward, we'd been seen by a policeman neither of us had detected. The character of the manhunt changed. State Police, FBI, and National Guardsmen poured in from all over as a perimeter was established around Gobbler's Knob.

They knew for certain now that I was still alive, and in the company of a murderer.

Chapter 6

We moved. More than ever before, I was threatened, spat upon, beaten, cursed, and perpetually kept moving. If I didn't keep moving, I'd be shot like that man in the clearing.

Then just shoot me! I almost wanted to scream. For the past week, I had been pummeled, kicked, bound, starved, and trained to believe that my family was dead to me, and I to them – if they were still alive at all. I was far beyond hungry and tired, becoming almost somnolent. I just wanted it all to end.

But I didn't ask to die. Instead, I kept shuffling one boot in front of the other. The mysterious voice, my only comfort over the past week, was still telling me to keep going, and that I'd be okay.

At a guess, sometime since the weekend my class ring slipped off my finger. It had fit the day I was taken. I never noticed its absence.

I remember, then, being up on Gobbler's Knob, looking south. There was activity on the roads that made the kidnapper angry. Below us was US Route 522 and just beyond that the Turnpike, so close that we could hear the oblivious trucks.

Bicycle Pete seemed to make up his mind.

"We're getting down there," he decided. "See that? That's the Turnpike. That's the Golden Egg." Agitated, he grabbed my face in both hands, ranting just as he had so often before, over and over again. "It's the Golden Egg! Do you understand what I'm telling you, bitch? It's the *Golden Egg!*"

Again we moved. Darkness fell. And Bicycle Pete, so accustomed to his life moving at a walking pace with time to observe everything around him in fine detail, missed something.

It was some hours after midnight, I'd guess, when we stopped in a sawmill, one of several scattered though the valley. They aren't always large operations, often just a few sheds in a clearing by a dirt road. It seemed a good place to hole up for the few minutes he'd stay anywhere.

The big sawdust pile was slowly rotting in the damp weather, and its vapor rose thick that night. I blinked. I hadn't been mistaken. There was a man there, a man made of the mist, standing on top of the pile. He had on a robe, his arms outstretched. I could make out his long hair and beard, but any features were indistinct, to the point that I didn't think he had a face at all.

Then I heard him, and knew the voice for the one I'd been hearing for the last several days.

You'll be all right, he said in that comforting voice. *You've been faithful. You've done well. Soon you'll be fine.*

Then I blinked again and the vision was gone, before I could thank Him. I knew then Who it was.

The kidnapper didn't hear or see the figure, or he would have shot at him; nor did he notice me looking. I didn't say anything. The voice had spoken to me, not to my captor.

What I hadn't seen that night was the cordon placed along Route 522 near Burnt Cabins. Police, National Guard, fire trucks and private vehicles were strung head to tail, engines running and headlights on, and everyone awake and watching despite the hour and the fumes. But we didn't try to cross the road that night, and I was in no shape by then to notice much of anything. Everything I had left was funneled into the overwhelming task of moving, of keeping up. It was futile now to hope that the kidnapper wouldn't be angry at me.

We set off from the sawmill after a few minutes. Since the heavy chain had been lost, a smaller, shorter one – a heavy dog leash or long choke collar – was looped tightly around my right wrist.

We crossed a ridge line and a field. I had been reassured by God's voice in the night, but by contrast the kidnapper seemed more nervous and volatile than ever before. As we hurried across the open field he frantically tore off the canvas bag he'd worn all this time, raging that it only had junk in it and how could he kill anyone with it getting in the way?

I was too far gone to feel any shock over the fact that Bicycle Pete had actually thrown away possessions.

In the gray dawn, we came upon a cabin at the foot of the knob, not too far from the highway, somewhere between Burnt Cabins and Fort

Littleton. Along that stretch there are places where the Turnpike is only a few yards from 522.

There was a car sitting there at the cabin. Inside the building, we both heard someone stirring.

Bicycle Pete took his little revolver out of his pocket. The cabin had an attached bathroom with the door on the outside. He tried it. It was unlocked. He shoved me inside, then closed the door behind himself and waited. Only two or three minutes passed until a man opened the door and saw Bicycle Pete.

"You're him! You're the kidnapper!" yelled the man, turning to run.

Bicycle Pete didn't hesitate. He pulled the trigger without aiming, hitting the man's midsection. The shot began to wake me up, dispersing the fog that had kept me alive for days. Someone else had been shot, someone asking me if he was badly hurt. I didn't know and couldn't answer, or I knew I'd have been shot too. I only saw the blood welling out of him.

"Get in the car," ordered Bicycle Pete. "You're driving me out of here."

"I'm bleeding!"

"*I don't care if you die! Get in the car!*"

The man was in his pajamas, with no shirt, but he had his keys with him. I was crammed face-up onto the back floor and Bicycle Pete simply climbed in over me, his feet holding me down and my own feet jammed up against the driver's-side door. The engine caught and we were off.

If we stopped at all on the way down, I truly don't remember. I do remember the car thumping across a timber bridge, and stopping, and the driver getting out. Then he was shouting to someone I couldn't see that *it's him, they're in the car* and *I've been shot* – something like that.

I could see nothing as the shooting started, lying helpless on my back on the car floor. Then Bicycle Pete lunged over me to the door and jumped out, literally pulling me up and out by the chain around my wrist.

"Run, bitch! You're going to get us both killed!" The car's back end was still over the bridge, but there was just enough room for us to get out onto the road and down the embankment to the stream.

It was then that for the first time, after surviving the entire week's ordeal, my ankle twisted.

Pain shot through me, but only for an instant; then I could run again. Still, it was an instant, and maybe it held him up long enough. He dragged me behind some sheds, up a dip in the ground from the stream to a gate by a barn. It was unlocked; we went through it, and were only a few feet from the hard road.

The commotion was only increasing. There was shouting, there were shots, and there were more people and cars coming, more than we'd seen all week, all focused on us. A helicopter came, hovering over the treeline across the road from the barn, drowning out everything else.

All the confusion overwhelmed him. I sensed that the demons that had driven this man for the past week were deserting him, leaving behind a simple, hunched Bicycle Pete, afraid and desperate, and now panicking.

"Get across the road!" he screamed at me. I ran across 522 ahead of Bicycle Pete's shotgun, against the blast of wind from the helicopter's rotors. It made the loudest noise I'd ever heard, and I still remember thinking how dangerously close it was to the top of a tall pine as we reached the house and ran alongside it. I was sure it was going to catch us by landing on us, or blowing us off our feet, if it didn't wreck against the tree first.

Somehow, I heard a steady voice coming

clearly from the helicopter above. "She's on the right, he's on the left. He's going down."

Down he went. Suddenly the weight was gone from my wrist, and I took the first chance at escape I'd had all that week, running away from him as hard as I could and heading right around the rear corner of the house, then straight for the back door. I must have passed someone, but that wasn't important. The back door wouldn't open. I wedged myself as tightly as I could between the screen door and the locked one, pounding on it until my hands were black and blue, crying to be let in before Bicycle Pete came around that corner to kill me or take me away again.

That was how two FBI agents found me. I begged them not to take me back around the side of the house where the kidnapper was. I was terrified, fully convinced that he would get up and shoot me and everybody else. But they reassured me that he was dead, that he couldn't hurt anyone anymore, and led me around the crowd gathering by the body. Bicycle Pete lay curled up into a fetal position and didn't move.

Just as God's voice had told me, it was over, and I was alive.

Chapter 7

There's a telephoto picture that appeared in the papers that day, of me staggering along 522 between two FBI agents, dressed in a too-large man's jacket and pants and rubber boots. In the background is the Rubeck's bank barn. The agents are Hal Briner and Finbar O'Connor. They were assigned as bodyguards, for lack of a better word. They became my constant companions for many days, and friends for years after.

They sat me between them in the back seat of a police cruiser, and we were off, but something wasn't right. "Where are we going?" I asked anxiously. "I just want to go home!" I was scared and bewildered, and the first thing I wanted was to know that my family was okay. I'd be all right if I could just go home. There wasn't anything wrong with me that a little time at home with soap and water wouldn't fix. But the police car was going the wrong way, very fast, with red lights and sirens running.

Instead of my house, they took me to McConnellsburg, to the Fulton County Medical Center, where a huge fuss was made over me. Disoriented and in shock, I was as terrified there as I had been in the mountains for the entire previous week. It felt nothing like a rescue.

First, they cut off the clothing – no surprise there, nothing would have been worth saving of my dress or blouse after that week.

I told them that it was unnecessary to examine me for rape, but they went ahead anyway. To my way of thinking they did worse to me that morning than I had suffered from the kidnapper. They performed an invasive, humiliating procedure over my protests and without even my parents' knowledge.

The conclusion was that there was long-dried semen on the inside of his pants, as I recall – the autopsy report said the same of the two pairs of pants the kidnapper had on when his body was examined, a few hours later – and that there was blood on me, but I had been in the midst of my period. It seemed to surprise a lot of people then, and still does now, that I had not been molested, exactly as I told the doctors. I suppose some policy required the exam, but I still don't think it was right to have done that to me, a minor, without my consent or the consent or presence of my parents.

In short order, I'd been examined, treated, and cleaned up. I'm not sure what it was, but they gave me something to help me calm down and relax. I was still on the gurney and had barely been covered back up with just a sheet when two men intruded into the examination room. I don't recall their faces at all; I only remember that they wore suits, not uniforms.

"Was there any sexual assault?" asked one immediately.

"*No*," said Dr. Lorenz shortly. "You have a few minutes. She's been through enough." With my family doctor on one side of me and the tiny figure of Nurse Marie Henry on the other, patting my shoulder and telling me that it was okay, they began.

"How do you feel?" (all right, I guess) – "Do you know what day this is?" (no) – "Do you know what happened?" (yes? No? Just to me, you mean?)

– "Do you remember where you went?" (I don't know; we went all over the place . . .)

I was becoming even more intimidated and bewildered by the vague probing. Couldn't they ask anything outright and specific that I could answer?

"What about *him*?"

"I . . . guess he's no longer with us?" Something about their manner must have made me think that they were talking about a dead man, but they didn't say who they were asking about – the kidnapper? The man in the clearing? The man who had been shot that morning? Hadn't he survived?

I began to cry. I just wanted my Mom, not these strangers who couldn't ask a straight question or tell me anything useful.

According to Nurse Henry, the reporters got their information then, but I don't know if they saw me at all. I remember that Dr. Lorenz cut everyone off and wheeled me across the hall to a private room. At the door stood two friendly faces, the FBI agents who had brought me in. "Are you okay?" they asked me. At least I could answer that.

The nurses slid me into a hospital bed, arranging the covers as a tent over my feet, which were to have nothing unnecessary touching them for the next week or so. I didn't get out of the bed at all for the next three days.

But just then, I wanted to see Mom and Dad and my brothers and sisters; where were they? I was assured that they were fine, but I couldn't believe that until I saw them. Until my parents walked into the room I wasn't sure that it was all really true, and that they were safe.

But then, there they were, alive and well. I couldn't take in that fact. I felt disconnected from them and from the whole surreal situation I found myself in, certain that in a moment I'd wake up to the screaming, contorted face of Bicycle Pete and the weight of the chain around my neck. That dreamlike feeling, thinking that I could be reentering my worst nightmare in the next instant, would not dispel for days.

No doubt I seemed distant and quiet, but I was so very thankful that I didn't have to tell my mother, the best mother in the whole world, that I'd been raped by that man, or even touched like that by him. I couldn't have hidden that from her, or lived with such a fact. Mom told me later, though, that she knew immediately upon hearing me talking to the nurses, before she even saw me, that that was one thing she didn't have to worry about.

Mom was still hugging me when I looked up and said, "I'm all right, Dad."

"I knew you would be," he replied. I don't remember the rest of my family visiting that morning but I know that they did.

After everything that had happened, I still couldn't sleep. I remember venting, talking to Agent O'Connor for a long while that day. I'd barely spoken a word for a whole week.

Almost the first thing he said to me was, "Did you ever know who he was?"

I didn't. Aside from "Bicycle Pete," I'd never had a name to put to the kidnapper.

"His name was Hollenbaugh," said Finbar O'Connor. "Bill Hollenbaugh."

In 1966 there were no HIPAA regulations about patients' private information; the medical profession was expected to be discreet, but with no mandate to be utterly secretive. The papers could report that my injuries were minor and that there had been no rape. Despite the truth of all this, I was kept in the hospital for thirteen days.

I was terribly dehydrated, and some fourteen pounds lighter than I'd been the week before. My face was black and blue. It's a miracle that I hadn't lost an eye forging through the underbrush with my hands tied. I hadn't lost any teeth (though even after fifty years my lower front teeth are still a little loose). There didn't seem to be anything they could do about my broken nose, but I could breathe okay so it wasn't too bad. The marks of the heavy chain didn't fade from my neck for a very long time, and my left side has been a little weaker than it should be ever since being battered with Bicycle Pete's fist and the chain it held. My hips were bruised and scraped from being kicked and repeatedly falling with bound hands.

The worst injuries, though, were to my feet and lower legs. The welts and scrapes on my legs had actually begun to heal a little since Saturday, when I'd had to put on the pants and boots; not so my feet.

My feet, with so much skin worn off the soles, had been trapped in those filthy boots for days, often enough with dirty water squelching around inside. They were badly infected, bearing huge blisters, and at one point the doctors feared that gangrene was setting in. I overheard two of them talking and bluntly asked the one who came to check on me what was going on. Two of my toes, he replied, were in bad shape; if the infection got worse they'd need to amputate.

"You won't have to," I told him. "I prayed it away. They'll get better."

He gave me an odd look. "You really do believe in God, don't you?"

I did. I had every reason to. Convalescing in bed, I had plenty of time to pray and plenty to pray about. And my feet did indeed get better; they remain scarred, but I still have all my toes.

The stay in the hospital was an adventure all its own. I had gone to a hospital once before, for an outpatient procedure. I'd never spent a night in one since my birth, and unless something was wrong we never went to a doctor, since we had a tight budget and no insurance.

For the first few days there, I was terrified that Bicycle Pete wasn't dead, and that he'd come to get me again. After that ordeal I really did not believe that he *could* die, much less that he really had been killed. It took perhaps three days before the overwhelming fear and the shock wore off, and I grew accustomed to my new surroundings. It was only then that the pain of my injuries finally hit me, though the only thing I remember taking was some aspirin. After the fear faded, the worst thing was the boredom.

That was alleviated a little by schoolwork. I

had a week's worth to catch up on, plus what I was missing by being in the hospital. Two of my teachers, Mr. Fraker and Mr. Baker, started bringing me my books and assignments within a day of my rescue. I'd do the work, and Dad would drop it off at the high school the day after. They immediately told me not to worry about my grades, that I'd pass that year anyway, but I didn't see any reason not to try for more than just a passing grade – indeed, there were lots of good reasons for me to do better. That hadn't changed.

A few days afterward, they brought me something else: they'd gotten my class ring replaced. The old one must still be out there somewhere, and has never been found to my knowledge.

Still, time lay heavy on me, especially the days while I was bed-bound. There was no television or radio in my hospital room, and McConnellsburg is still a quiet place, as it was then. The silence was all but absolute for hours on end, except for the staff poking their heads in to see if I needed anything. Some days there were so many such inquiries that I wondered if I was the only patient there.

When I progressed to a wheelchair and then

to walking, still with pain despite specially cushioned tennis shoes, I took to visiting other patients and making friends.

All this time I had company. Agent Briner was stationed outside my door, with Agent O'Connor in my room. When the nurses came by to care for me those first few times, they treated me like glass. "You know that he has to stay in the room, don't you?" they asked nervously, even as they drew the curtains around the bed.

Puzzled, I said something like, "He's a gentleman; he can turn his head." He was both a gentleman and a professional, and did so.

Naturally, like any well-brought-up girl, I'd very much have preferred for him to step outside, but he couldn't. As time wore on, he and Agent Briner became friends with myself and with Mrs. Henry, the RN who had been on duty when I was admitted and who had taken me under her wing. Both agents reiterated to me, as often as I needed to hear it, that the kidnapper was dead and couldn't come back for me.

Obviously, I had been out of touch for a week, and wasn't used to seeing a newspaper or watching TV news anyway, so I had no idea how much attention was being paid to *me* in addition to the criminal and the crime itself. I'd only glimpsed the scale of the manhunt over the past week. With all that over and done, I thought the whole thing should blow over in a few days.

On the second day in the hospital, Thursday, I overheard Dr. Lorenz and my father talking to someone outside my door early in the morning. It didn't make much sense to me at that time when I heard the doctor say something like, "You tell them that *she* has no deadline. She'll be ready to talk when *I* say she's ready, and she's not ready yet." Dad backed him up in no uncertain terms. But I couldn't see who they were talking to, if it wasn't Agent Briner. Were they talking about Mom? Why? No, they told me, it wasn't about my mother; but they didn't tell me what it *was* about. I now have reason to believe that they were talking about police or reporters, or both.

The result of the doctor's refusal to allow an interview that day, however justified by his patient's condition, has haunted (or at least pestered) me ever since – even if I didn't realize it for a long time. Aside from those few distressing and confusing minutes on the morning I was admitted, I don't recall formally talking to law enforcement while in the hospital.

A beautician from McConnellsburg visited

me every day for those first few days. My hair had fallen to about shoulder-length when I'd left school last Wednesday, but since then it had been yanked, soaked, dried, windblown, and tangled in leaves and branches and bark and just plain dirt. Upon seeing me Mom had begged the staff not to let me see myself in a mirror – as if my mere appearance could distress me after surviving such a week. This lady did a wonderful job, however, and didn't have to cut much off. She finished right in time for a much-anticipated event: a television news crew from Pittsburgh came to interview me that Saturday.

The minister from my church, Reverend Piper, read a statement for me that I'd composed:

> *"It would be easy to say that I despise the very memory of the Mountain Man and let it go at that. But I don't believe that all the misery, sorrow and death he caused was entirely his fault, any more than it is a snake's fault when it strikes someone who steps on it. I'll leave it to the psychiatrists to diagnose what was wrong with his mind, but it seemed to me that he was a person everybody had rejected, not tried to help. Apparently*

nobody ever took an interest in him. He was about as lonely as a human being can get. So he was fighting back in the only way he could figure out, trying to capture by force the human companionship he couldn't get any other way. I just happened to be the one he caught."

The original is long lost, but it ran something like that, although I don't remember saying anything about snakes. (Since I didn't see the newspapers, it was a long while before I was aware that it sparked uninformed comments about how uncaring the community had been, and provoked rebuttals from the people who had tried to befriend Hollenbaugh and were ignored or rebuffed.)

Aside from that, I don't remember talking to any reporters, although they were resorting to trickery to sneak in. I heard of some tagging along with the sick or injured, or with patients' families.

On one of those first few unsettled days, I spotted a movement at my window. A hand was gripping the window sill. For a moment, terror flashed through me: was it Bicycle Pete, come to take me away again, or to kill me for escaping him? At that point I still didn't really believe that he could have died. I managed to draw Agent O'Connor's attention.

"There's somebody out there," I whispered.

He poked his head out the door, and Agent Briner sauntered off. Then Agent O'Connor sidled along the wall, threw up the sash and chopped at the straining fingers on the sill with his hand.

There was a yell. My room was on the second floor.

Agent O'Connor looked down at the bushes beneath the window. "Now we'll know who he is – oh, there, he's getting apprehended."

He turned back to me. "It wasn't Hollenbaugh. He can't come back to hurt you." That was when he told me, "There must be a lot going around inside that pretty head of yours. Anything you ever want to say, it won't leave this room." I think, on the very first day of our acquaintance, he may possibly have repeated some things I said to a superior; after all, they'd lost an agent the day before, and I was there to see it. But I also think, once he made that promise to me, that both agents kept it.

Both he and Agent Briner stuck around longer than they were originally supposed to, thanks to people trying stunts like the man at my widow. At last, though, they could turn in their final reports, and go home.

Fulton County Medical Center wasn't a big hospital. They were well-equipped to handle my injuries, but they simply didn't have anywhere to accommodate all the flowers, stuffed animals, and bric-a-brac that began to arrive for me. My room was full. The hallways and lobby were crowded to the point that the staff had difficulty getting around to do their jobs. Dad had to bring the station wagon to remove all he could; we ended up giving a lot of it away – to the hospital staff, other patients, nursing homes, churches, anywhere that would take it. Our house wasn't big enough to hold it all, and things kept coming, from all over the country and all over the world.

Some things we did keep, of course. I was surprised to receive a number of medals and other small items from servicemen, especially ones stationed in Vietnam. I ran across a local veteran years later who explained why he had sent me his medal: it seems that a seventeen-year-old, yanked away from her home and family and dragged through the wilderness by a maniac for a week, and surviving, resonated with them. I gave them hope that they would come home, and they paid me back with what luck they could send.

Other things were more tangible. Most notable was the package from President and Mrs. Johnson – a new dress, the best I'd ever seen, of a simple style that might be in fashion for some time yet. It was dark blue with a white panel in front. With it came matching pumps and a pearl necklace and earrings: the basic necessities of a good turnout. For a young woman of such limited means who was suddenly being pushed into the spotlight, it was a very thoughtful, practical gift. I wore it home from the hospital.

Empire Beauty School gave me something even more lasting: a scholarship, including a transportation allowance. Because of that I earned my cosmetologist's license in good time, and with the money I saved because of it I eventually moved away.

A few other things stand out in my memory. Two summers before, I'd spent a few weeks away from home, helping an uncle in his store while my aunt had an operation. One of their neighbors was a young man with a car who began to hang around for a glimpse of me. "Doesn't he have a job?" I'd asked my uncle, incredulous.

As it turned out, he didn't. He was the son of a local lawyer, home for the summer from his freshman year at one of the Ivy League colleges.

My aunt sighed a bit over the fact that I really was too young to be dating yet, but there it was.

While I was in the hospital, he sent me a bouquet and a card. With grace and good humor he apologized for his behavior that summer, and said he was glad I was all right.

Not everybody's attention was so appreciated. A tip for the gentlemen: whoever you are, whether the King or a Royal Highness, any offer to a young woman in my position to come visit you is only going to make you appear a total creep.

I'm sure the hospital was glad to see the last of me. I doubt they'd ever needed security guards before, and probably never have that badly since.

Chapter 8

I was discharged from the Fulton County Medical Center on May 31, 1966, and went home.

It wasn't the end of anything.

When I went up to the girls' bedroom, it was a great deal emptier than I'd left it three weeks before. Clothes from the laundry and bedding that I'd slept on had been taken for their scent, for the tracking dogs; that wasn't unexpected. But where were the clean clothes, the cosmetics, the little jewelry I'd owned? The comb, hairbrush and hair rollers? Of all things, the bobby pins?

Dad and the rest of my family had suffered a far different experience with the police, and especially with the FBI, than I had. To him, the

State Police seemed to have gotten off to a slow start. I learned that they had initially suspected Gene Clippinger, whose house was a few hundred yards from where I was taken. He passed a polygraph test, of course, and after questioning Dick Miller and Isaac Frehn too, they'd finally fixed on the right man – but if they'd listened to a frightened nine-year-old girl as well as Mr. Clippinger had, they would have known that there simply wasn't time for him or for elderly Mr. Miller to kidnap me before my sister Debbie found them at their homes. Simple logic would have left Mr. Frehn out of the picture; he still had kids on the bus, and it would have taken their complicity and that of their families and mine to conceal the crime.

The task of guarding my family seems to have fallen, partly at least, on the shoulders of State Trooper Tom Ruegg. He was a sensible man with a military background similar to Dad's. He took good care of the children and got along with the adults – but then the FBI had come.

"Think about it," Dad said. "Some of them acted like they had never been away from town. There were FBI agents who were afraid to step out of their cars and walk into the woods. So they settled on the easiest explanation." By Dad's account they had wasted three or four days, insisting that Dad didn't know his teenage daughter and that I had run off with some boy I'd been seeing in my spare time.

"What spare time?" Dad had argued bluntly. "She's here. I drive her to her work and pick her up afterwards. She comes straight home on the bus with the other kids." The rare times I'd gone anywhere that spring were with Darlene Mentzer, who was an adult, except for that Wednesday when Mrs. Keith had arranged to pick me up for the fashion show. (For the record, the fashion show went on as planned on May 11th. My suit was displayed, and an announcement was made about the kidnapping, expressing the hopes of all for my safe return. I was glad to know that my hard work hadn't gone to waste.)

For all my high school years I had fulfilled my responsibilities at home, taking care of my siblings and the house while my parents worked long shifts at canneries, working myself, and keeping my grades up. I had no time to be the rebellious teenage girl that the highest authorities present told Dad that I must be – as if I'd have gone anywhere with any boy I knew who had pointed a gun at my family!

I learned long after the fact that a classmate whom I'd never liked, whose behavior at school would now be termed *stalking*, had shown up at the picnic grounds. He'd hung around the reporters, passing himself off as my devastated college freshman boyfriend, getting the attention he craved and his name in the papers. Even now I can't feel bad about the face-full of locker door I'd given him earlier in the school year.

The first suspects in a crime like this are usually from the family, and then from among neighbors, but we didn't know that then. While a few of the authorities were making themselves unpopular with my father, the hunt for Bicycle Pete had continued.

Two State Troopers from out of the area had been staking out his cabin on the evening we went there, but were later suspected of being asleep while on duty. In any case, they only saw us leaving, when we were by the treeline and Hollenbaugh shot at his dog, and I saw a man by the cabin. They claimed that I was chained to a tree while Hollenbaugh went by himself to feed the dogs, but he took me with him and never left me alone. We didn't see the police car either, since we approached from the field behind the buildings.

That turned out to be the first real indication to the police that the search was still for a living victim, not a corpse.

The farmhouse we'd entered the following night belonged to an older couple, the McKenzies. I heard later that at least one other cache of food and other loot had been found in a nearby sawmill's slab pile. The events were conflated, and one account has me lugging sheet-loads (plural) of swag up a mountainside from the McKenzie's house – as if Hollenbaugh would have taken anything except a gun that wouldn't fit into his pockets, or taken the time and the ludicrous risk of being seen looting a house located right on the bend of a well-used road during the manhunt.

On the Tuesday morning after that, the resident agent from the Harrisburg FBI field office invited himself out with Troopers George Plafcan and Howard Parlett, dog trainer Tom McGinn and three tracking dogs, dog handler Jack Staud from New York, and Lloyd Fogal who now owned the family farm near which Hollenbaugh's cabin sat. Special Agent Terry Ray Anderson was to have monitored the radio from the vehicle they set up as a command post. Instead, he took the portable radio with its shoulder strap from Trooper Parlett, and took that man's place in the party.

A short time later, Trooper Parlett had to relay the news that Agent Anderson had been shot and killed.

Terry Anderson was the man I'd seen Hollenbaugh shoot that morning. It would surely have been more prudent of Anderson to remain behind and allow someone with a better sense of these woods to go along, as had been planned. But he was like that, by all accounts: active, aggressive, focused on finding the victim – me – and catching the perpetrator, and he had handled dogs while serving in the Marine Corps.

Weid was the first dog sent into the brush when the shooting started, and was himself killed; the other dog I saw, that McGinn handled, was shot but recovered. The third dog was never released. Decades later someone told me that he turned on his handler when they returned without his comrades.

The man that Hollenbaugh shot at the cabin on Gobbler's Knob that Wednesday morning was Francis Sharpe, a deputy from Cambria County. In defiance of the State Troopers guarding the section of 522 at the Rubeck farm, he had crossed the perimeter and gone to get a good night's sleep at a place owned by friends of his, the Shoneks. He recovered from his wound, serious as it was. I still keep in touch with his daughter.

I eventually met the State Troopers who had been at the Rubeck's: Grant Mixell and Richard Bodine from Carlisle. One of them asked, "Peggy, do you know what happened to that chain?"

I didn't know. I only knew that it had dropped off my wrist, and then I had run. No one ever admitted to finding it, to my knowledge. I have always believed that God made it vanish.

Of course, Dad always thought that someone came out of the situation richer by one good dog collar.

While I was in the hospital, I had only caught snippets of the events. I don't recall anyone ever thoroughly interviewing me in any detail, much less telling me everything I missed, so there are things I still haven't heard. There are pieces of the puzzle missing for me fifty years later, and others only now falling into place.

I am very grateful that, of all the things that could have haunted me, I have never suffered nightmares. What I can't take are pieces of clothing or jewelry that fit tightly about the neck or wrist, or anyone gripping me there.

Maybe the worst effect of the captivity upon me was slow to fade: for a long time, the sight of anyone bearing even a slight resemblance to Bicycle Pete would send me hurrying the other way. One of the first people who affected me this way was Tom McGinn, the dog trainer whose dogs were shot as I watched. It may be prejudice but I remember that there were other things about his manner that I didn't like, however well-regarded he was by the men he worked with that week. This feeling persists despite the sacrifices he made to find me. Among other things, I heard that he may never have been paid for his services or for the two dogs that were shot, and that he returned home to find that he'd been fired because of his absence.

I didn't have to do a lot of talking about the ordeal after the next week was over, but that week was a trial.

I went back to school on June first. I'd been looking forward to riding the bus with my friends and being normal again – but that was not to be.

On that morning, one familiar face and one stranger, at least to me, arrived at our door. FBI

Special Agent Hal Briner was by now a great friend, and I was introduced to his associate. "I'm glad to meet you at last," I remember Trooper Tom Ruegg saying.

I had to go to school in a State Police car with Tom Ruegg driving and Agent Briner with me in the back. I couldn't attend classes but was ushered straight into the empty library. Trooper Ruegg stood guard at the door and Agent Briner was in the room with me. All that was left that year for me was finals, anyway. For the rest of the week I'd take a test or two and then leave for the day.

In the car one afternoon they turned the radio on for me. Someone had recorded a song about the kidnapping, and we listened, and . . . well, fifty years later I heard that the artist was more or less coerced into the project by the record company. That makes me feel a little better. All the same, I signed 45's of "Eight Days at Shade-y Gap" up at McCrory's in Huntingdon for a day later that summer. If they wanted so little of me as signing records, I could do that after everything that everyone had done for me.

Those first several afternoons, though, were another sort of test. I had to testify about my experiences before Judge Himes at the courthouse in Huntingdon. He said that I didn't need a lawyer, which I couldn't have afforded anyway; he said that I had a State Trooper and an FBI agent to look after me.

Nowadays, I'm sure he couldn't have gotten away with that. There should have been legal representation available for minors in such a position. Neither the State Police nor the FBI could do anything for me by way of legal counsel, although they did what they could.

Judge Himes, whose path I would cross again years later under friendlier circumstances, was not pleasant. He grilled me for those four days, picking apart my performance over that week I'd spent in Hollenbaugh's presence, seemingly trying to get me to admit to some sort of complicity in the crime. He said at the outset something about confirming what he'd read or heard about. I assumed he meant the newspapers.

I wanted to tell him loudly and firmly that *yes, you'd trespass too if someone held a sawed-off shotgun to you. You wouldn't run away unless you wanted to get shot and die, and you couldn't if you were chained. You couldn't fight a shotgun and a locked chain and a stronger man with bare hands. You wouldn't argue or speak at all if you were smart.*

Once or twice, Trooper Ruegg and Agent Briner saw that I was really upset. They cut a session or two short despite the judge, and took me over to Grubb's Diner for ice cream before taking me home.

The last thing I said to the judge was, "You never asked what happened to that apple."

"No," he said, taken aback.

"I don't know," I told him. After that week's interrogation, I was left with the feeling that if I'd eaten it and told him so, he'd have had me charged with the theft. Bicycle Pete had taken care of that though, by throwing the apple away when I wouldn't take it.

Judge Himes stated, after that last session, that I was nobody's fool. It was a compliment.

Things eventually settled down a bit. The police stayed with us for the summer, ticketing tourists and sightseers before Dad could throw them off the property. The clothing and supplies I'd lost quickly got replaced, thanks in large part to a group of women who canvassed Orbisonia and Rockhill for donations of clothes. None of my things were returned that I remember.

The Saturday Evening Post interviewed me for about ten minutes, soon after I left the hospital.

107

The journalist asked a few questions that had nothing to do with the actual abduction, dressed up the story as it had been told in the papers, and took me down to the bridge by the McKenzie farm for a picture, all made up like some movie star. The photographer had me put my red scarf over my hair because of the wind. I never wore scarves that way, and in the picture I look serious. Actually, I was tired by then and my patience had worn very thin. (*Life Magazine* didn't send anyone that I recall; they just rehashed the old material.)

Only recently have I read the *Daily News* article announcing an arrangement between my parents and *The Saturday Evening Post*. The price for the exclusive rights to my story wasn't revealed, and I never thought that any money was involved; but since the contract was handled by a law firm acting on my parents' behalf, the magazine must have paid enough to cover the lawyer, at least. Upon reflection, though, I now think that there was more. We were still struggling financially after I left the hospital – but no more than we had before I was kidnapped, spent two weeks recovering in a small medical center with no health insurance, and before Mom missed a week or more of work while needing Dr.

Lorenz to visit daily. I wonder if the price for the story was that the magazine paid the medical and legal bills, perhaps without my parents even seeing the money.

However, such a stink was raised in the paper about my story being sold (and my parents handling money rightfully belonging to their minor daughter) that Judge Himes appointed a local banker as my financial guardian. What remained in that account eventually helped with my expenses at beauty school, and to make my first home livable.

What makes sense to me is that my parents could not refuse every offer they received for the story. They had no way to pay for my recovery. No paper reported any effort to raise funds for my expenses that I've ever read. Offered such a deal from a reputable magazine, in the face of all the inaccuracies appearing in the papers, my parents might have thought that selling the story to the *Post* was the best solution to both problems.

If so, it only solved one. Had the writer spent even a few hours asking me what had happened, rather than a few minutes, the story would have taken a far different form.

Life moved on. Later that summer, a man stopped to visit Mom and Dad. It was Mr.

Cornelius, an elderly man who owned a furniture store on the way to McConnellsburg. He had wanted to help with the search, but had been unable to leave his business, his only source of income, unattended. We were flabbergasted by the offer he made.

"I want you to come to my store," he told Mom. "Pick out anything you like from the floor displays. Everything you need."

"I can't do that!" Mom exclaimed.

"I knew you'd say that," said Mr. Cornelius. "Yes, you can. If you don't, I'll still have to write it off and get rid of it somehow or other before the new stock comes in."

Somehow he convinced them. He gave us the first new furniture we'd ever had, from mattresses for the new bedsteads to a kitchen table and chairs to a couch, and everything to go with them, and brought it all to the house. It was so good to realize that people had been thinking of Mom and Dad too while I was gone.

It was in stark contrast to Mom's first day back at work in the cannery. Management did not confront her directly about her unauthorized absence. Instead, the supervisor sent his line-boss girlfriend to say that, since we were so rich now that Mom could take the whole week off while her daughter was away, they were surprised that she'd shown up.

"I wouldn't be here if I didn't need to work," Mom replied with dignity. "Do I stay, or am I fired?" She was allowed to stay, although she was still in tears when she came home.

That was only one instance of the unfounded notion that notoriety and tragedy equal a free living. For the record, that isn't true of me, my family, or the vast majority of survivors of anything, anywhere.

The rumor mill worked overtime then, and some stories persist about money. For one thing, there were people absolutely convinced that my father had orchestrated the entire thing for ransom, despite the lack of any money anywhere in the case, the lack of any ransom demand, or the investigations of the Law – and certainly despite anything I could say about the event.

A week or so after finals were done and the court depositions sealed, when my feet were finally up to the task, several State Policemen and National Guardsmen had me take them around to places I'd been taken by Hollenbaugh. It was done in bits over the course of several weeks. The woods had changed by then into full summer foliage, so much so that many of the places were all but totally unfamiliar and inaccessible; we had to revisit most locations later that fall, when the leaves were down. Eventually we found a lot of the caves and hiding places, including the one camouflaged by rocks cemented onto the door.

One man, Trooper Palmieri, fell and was badly injured. He was a big man and had to be carried out. He'd broken his back but, thankfully, he recovered fully.

We never did find the lard can with the papers and the pistol. The revolver is on display at the State Police museum, so the lost gun must be the semiauto from the McKenzie's. If anyone ever runs across it, or has found anything else from one of the Mountain Man's hiding places, please turn it in to the Pennsylvania State Police. The case cannot be closed until the evidence we know is still out there is accounted for, including the .30-.30 rifle that he used to shoot Ned Price.

That summer passed unlike any before or since. There were State Police going through my mail – there were bags of that, some of it hate mail. We were guarded until sometime around the start of school, when the police officially concluded that Hollenbaugh had acted alone and moreover was solely responsible for several burglaries: four businesses in one night a few years before when he'd gotten the .30-.30, the shotgun that he modified, and the Philco radio, and another break-in at Himes' Jewelers. They'd found some of the missing jewelry under the floorboards of his cabin. The police believed that he gave it away as gifts to family members, but it was shiny and expensive, and like the gun he took from the McKenzies, some of it may have been rather a trophy to hoard or a resource to pawn.

I can't remember how or from whom I recall hearing that they found a set of orange coveralls there, but it brought to mind the hunter that ran from Jim one evening as he went up the hill to adjust the TV antenna.

Naturally there was a huge change in our attitudes toward the police. Once, they'd been "hogs" and no one wanted to tell them a thing. Now, whenever they were in the area, they'd stop by to see how we were.

One day a trooper came to the door and asked Dad how he was doing. "I'm doing okay," Dad said to him, then added, "I quit drinking."

It was the first time I'd ever heard him admit

that there had been a problem. It was true; despite the shakes and the cravings, he'd quit cold turkey. It probably saved both his life and my parents' marriage.

The day that school started, I was met outside the building by principals Mr. Yetter and Mr. Angle, and Mr. Blair Shore, a *Daily News* photographer. The principals presented me with a gift from my classmates: a gorgeous white sweater to replace the one I'd lost. On it was a dragonfly pin from my teachers, and there was a bracelet, a loosely-fitting chain of oval stones. Mom and Dad were there, and there are pictures, with my big stack of books split between Dad and myself.

By that time, though, school and work had competition for my time and attention. The rest of my life was beginning.

Perspectives

Debbie Bradnick

Once, we were downstairs when Dad came in drunk and started in on Mom, and it got to be too much. One of us got between them.

"Dad! Stop it! Stop it, or something bad is going to happen to our family!" It turned out to be Peggy. She was brushed aside, and Dad didn't stop hitting Mom. We were afraid he'd kill her. But if the words meant anything, they applied just as much to what happened later that spring.

Around the same time, I stayed home sick for a day. Mom was out hanging up laundry and

I sat outside while she did. Up in the woods across the stream, there was a man sitting, watching the house. I pointed him out to Mom.

"Just a hunter," was her opinion.

An hour later he was still there, but Mom thought nothing of it and didn't want me to say anything more about it. So I didn't, even when I saw the man still out there hours later, around five that evening.

When we all got off the bus that one day, everybody but Peggy and Mary picked up rocks to throw, and we called them "prissy" for not joining in. There were four or so doe that would cross our lane just in front of us as we walked home, and this afternoon we'd decided that it would be a great thing to take one down with stones and bring it home to Dad: lots of fresh meat, courtesy of one sixteen-year-old with two nine-year-olds and an eight-year-old, and rocks. Well, we were kids.

Instead of the deer, though, there was a man behind a tree. The trunk was too skinny to hide him, but we figured him for a hunter after the same deer we wanted. Then he stepped out onto the roadway and pointed that shotgun at each of us in turn.

"I don't want any bullsh-t out of any of you," I remember him saying. The whole scene seemed to take forever to play out, the man in his thick green goggles looking over each one of us and eventually saying we were too young. I had been trailing behind the pack, and my brothers had been out in front. When the man reached Peggy, he said, "You're what I'm looking for. You can keep up." I thought he swatted her books down onto the road, but couldn't really see what happened because he grabbed her by the scruff of the neck and dragged her away through the woods.

If my sister said anything then, I didn't hear it; I probably couldn't have. What felt like an eternity probably only took a minute or less. Then Jimmy was running for home and Dad, and Mary was starting to follow with the other two. But that would take too long. I turned and ran back to the road.

The first house I came to was Dick Miller's, but as he said when I saw him and told him what happened, there wasn't anything he could do – a man in his eighties, no phone or car or anything. When we needed to make a call, we went to the next house. Gene Clippinger lived a few hundred feet up the road, and was a constable as well.

He believed me. He called the State Police, then tried to send me home. Of course I wouldn't go alone, so he put me in his car and drove me. When we got to where the kidnapping had taken place, there were Dad and Jimmy. Dad was angry, so angry that the top of his bald head was all red, calling for Peggy. Mr. Clippinger took us all back to our house, where Dad had all five of us kids get in our car, and we drove to go get Mom from where she was working that afternoon.

Mom was devastated, falling to her knees inside the house and crying. That evening, I think, and every day thereafter, Dr. Lorenz stopped by, and Mom mostly lay on a cot in the living room in the corner opposite the front door. I was too young to really appreciate that he was sedating my mother. Dad dragged a chair over by the door itself and sat there for the next week, hardly moving, never leaving home. Until the police persuaded him to put it up, he had his shotgun with him as he sat.

I don't remember who it was, but a woman came in to take care of us. Friends and relatives made sure we were fed. There were always one or two policemen on the front porch, keeping away anyone who had no business there, sharing their lunches with the white roosters who hopped up onto their knees and making sure that we kids worked off some energy caring for the animals and guarding us while we played ball or whatever in the flat space by the house.

Mom had never liked owls. For whatever reason, they were especially loud and active that week. Ever since then I've been terrified of owls hooting.

Monday or Tuesday we went back to school. I had no idea what was going on with the search, but it was decided that there was no reason to keep us out of classes any longer. I seem to remember police there, where they'd never been before.

We hadn't been in school very long on Wednesday morning when we were yanked out of class by a policeman saying, "We found your sister." We were packed into a police cruiser with its red bubble light going. As we neared Burnt Cabins, cars lined the road – along with police cruisers, fire engines, and army trucks; as we approached what I learned was the Rubeck farm, there were lots of ambulances. Up on the Turnpike there were cars pulled over, again lined up bumper to bumper. I've thought for a long time that I remembered hearing shots, but by that time the action was long over.

We kept on towards McConnellsburg, faster than I'd ever gone. I don't know when we got there, but Mom and Dad were there already; Mom was still a little out of it.

We couldn't stay long with Peggy that day, but she was a mess, even after they cleaned her up. I saw her legs, with the skin ripped up, and her feet were worse. Her face was black and blue. But my sister was alive.

[*According to Peggy, her sister Mary estimated that they had only been in school some ten or fifteen minutes on Wednesday May 18th when the police pulled them out of class.*]

Shirley Bair

My parents are Guy and Marie Price, and Mildred Moore was raised with me, so my Mom and Dad were Uncle Guy and Aunt Marie to her, and to her children; and I am their Aunt Shirley.

I remember that, back around the late 1950's, someone used to shoot at cars and trucks on the Turnpike for fun, but they caught him. It wasn't part of what Hollenbaugh did. He moved here later.

I remember being at home and hearing about Peggy being kidnapped. I picked up the phone and called my parents. Mom answered, and I asked to speak with Dad.

"What's wrong?" asked Mom.

"I need to talk to Dad," I repeated, and she went and got him. I told him what had happened and that I was going over there. Mom told me afterward never to scare her like that again.

When I got to the Bradnick house, there were cops and cop cars, and Gene sitting by the door, and Mid on the couch across the room. She was sedated enough to calm her down, not to put her out completely. For the next few days she had to have all the other children sitting on the couch with her, where she could see them.

After a few days, though, the police talked to her, and she let them outside long enough to play while the cops guarded them; and then the police took them back to school the next week. She tried to function enough to help in the kitchen, but in the midst of it she'd break down, sobbing "Why Peggy? Why my Peggy?"

The reporters were not polite. I answered a knock on the door once that weekend to find one there wanting pictures as the family sat down to eat supper. I refused, telling him to come back later. The police explained to me then that they couldn't prevent the press from knocking on our door, but that I or another family member had to tell them to go away. I hadn't known that.

Route 522 is the main highway through the valley. There was construction going on that spring, from the new bypass around Shade Gap to widening and straightening the road all the way to Burnt Cabins, but it stopped for that week and the road crews stayed away.

That next Wednesday morning, when we heard that Peggy had been found and was on her way to McConnellsburg, of course Mid and Gene went. My uncle Ned Price, who'd had his leg shot off, went roaring down to the Rubeck farm to see the body. Until Ned died, he never believed it was Hollenbaugh that shot him; he always said that the man he saw was over six feet tall, and that Hollenbaugh was a little shrimpy thing; and they never did find the gun that shot Ned's leg. But who knows how many places he had up in the mountains, where he stashed things?

The house rented by the Bradnicks in 1966 still stands in 2016, much as it was when these pictures were taken. *Above*, a view from the road; *below*, the chicken coop is across the lane. The bare tree trunk marks where the television antenna was placed. Note the edge of the jack pine thicket uphill to the right, where a watcher was startled into flight one evening. *Photos by Blair Shore, courtesy of Sandy Kleckner*

Above: Hollenbaugh's shack. The cabin sat above US 522; there is a long view of traffic in each direction. *Inset:* Best known pictures of Hollenbaugh, taken while in Farview and dated December 27, 1960. These were printed and passed out by the dozens to searchers, residents, and the press. *Below:* Two views inside the shack. Note the bicycle in the back room, which served as a bedroom. *Inset photos of William Hollenbaugh uncredited, all others by Blair Shore, courtesy of Sandy Kleckner.*

Left: State Police investigate the shooting of Ned Price at the Devlin house near Shade Gap. The Prices did not live in the house itself, but in a rented trailer on the property.

Right, left to right: Mrs. Devlin, Mrs. Jessie Price, Mrs. Shirley Bair await word of Mr. Price's condition. *Below:* Ned Price recovers in the hospital.

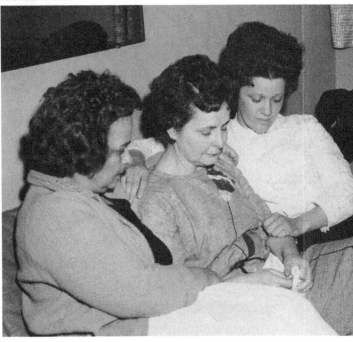

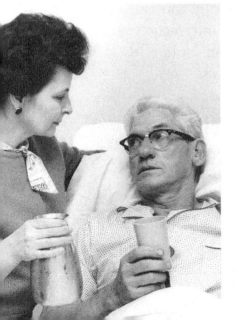

The apparently random selection of the victims, and the long intervals between spates of incidents, fueled speculation among residents that the culprit was foreign to the area rather than a resident. *Photos by Blair Shore, courtesy of Sandy Kleckner*

Above: Site of the abduction in 2016. Even in winter, it is difficult to see the ridge that slopes down from the left to end near the center of the photograph. Peggy was dragged straight ahead, east toward the ridge. *Below left*, the Mountain Man stood partially concealed behind one of these trees; *below right*, the intersection with Pleasant Hill Road is visible today, after Hollow Road has been widened. *Photos by Chris Armagost*

Above: Eugene and Mildred Bradnick soon after the kidnapping. *Photo by Blair Shore, courtesy of Sandy Kleckner.* *Below:* To Peggy, everything in this scene speaks about the family's way of life. What was not typical was the somber manner of her siblings *(left to right)* Donnie, Mary (seated), Carol Jean, and Debbie. *Photo by Ken Peiffer*

Above: Initial efforts to track the Mountain Man and Peggy were coordinated from the hood of a police cruiser parked outside the Bradnick residence. *Below*: The command post was transferred to Harper Memorial Park, employing facilities normally used for the Shade Gap Picnic. *Photos by Blair Shore, courtesy of Sandy Kleckner*

Above: A new U.S. Army Chinook helicopter taking off from the Shade Gap picnic grounds. Aircraft were used in the search and for transporting men and materials, such as current maps. *Below:* Volunteers from Juniata College in Huntingdon arrived Saturday morning. The student in the college shirt in the middle has been identified as Mr. Joseph Shull, at that time from neighboring Franklin County. *Photos by Blair Shore, courtesy of Sandy Kleckner*

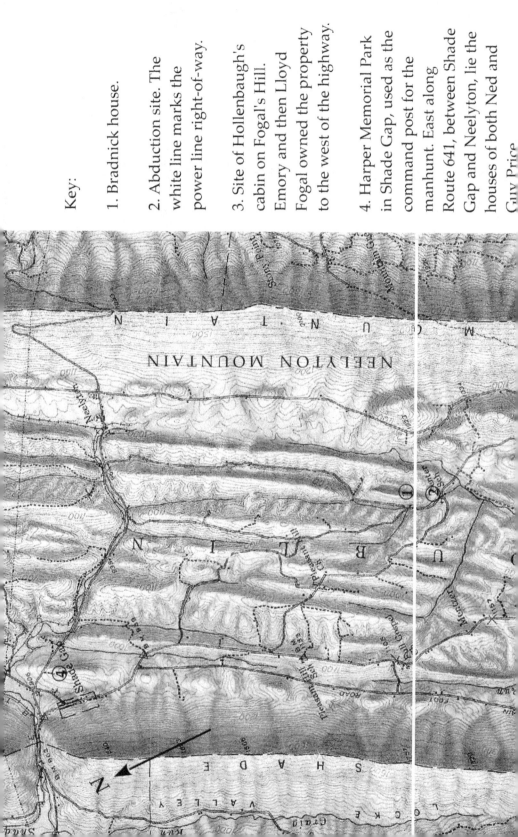

Key:

1. Bradnick house.

2. Abduction site. The white line marks the power line right-of-way.

3. Site of Hollenbaugh's cabin on Fogal's Hill. Emory and then Lloyd Fogal owned the property to the west of the highway.

4. Harper Memorial Park in Shade Gap, used as the command post for the manhunt. East along Route 641, between Shade Gap and Neelyton, lie the houses of both Ned and Guy Price.

5. Area of FBI Agent Terry Anderson's murder. The location is privately owned, and the owners have erected a small memorial marker.

6. Area containing a sawmill where the fugitive and victim paused, and the Shonek's cabin used by Deputy Francis Sharpe.

7. Rubeck farm, site of Hollenbaugh's death.

Map: US Dept. of the Interior, Geological Survey of 1939, shaded 1944 ed., courtesy of PASDA
Scale: Distance from Shade Gap to Burnt Cabins is approximately 8 mi.

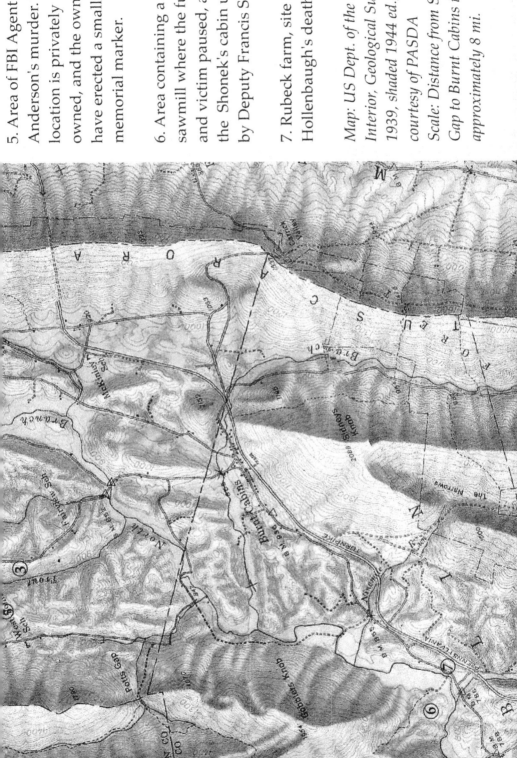

cing page: FBI Special Agent Terry Anderson's body is placed in an ambulance after reaching Hollenbaugh's cabin. *Below left:* Agent Anderson, standing, at the Shade Gap command post sometime before that search.
Below right: Dog trainer Tom McGinn with the body of his dog Weid, killed in the same action as Terry Anderson. *Photos by Blair Shore, courtesy of Sandy Kleckner*

Tuesday evening near Hollenbaugh's shack. The vehicles are on what is now US 522. *Photo by Blair Shore, courtesy of Sandy Kleckner*

Left: Sidney's Knob rises over the Shonek cabin. *Below*: The road from the cabin across the Rubeck's pasture to 522. The Turnpike runs behind the house. *Collection of P. Jackson.*

Above: Francis Sharpe drove over this bridge, calling for help as he opened the gate onto US 522. As two State Troopers opened fire, Hollenbaugh dragged his captive down to the creek and to the left. *Collection of P. Jackson.* *Below*, State Troopers in front of the Rubeck farmhouse. Hollenbaugh, with Peggy in front of him, ran from the barn (out of view to the left) across the road, falling by the bushes at the end of the house. The hole in the window where Larry Rubeck's shot shattered the glass is visible. *Photo by Blair Shore, courtesy of Sandy Kleckner*

Above left: One of the Mountain Man's camoflaged caves, Nov. 1966. *Above right*: The sandstone cave, only a few feet deep. *Collection of P. Jackson*

Above left: Peggy in front of the cave, with the door pulled aside. *Collection of P. Jackson. Above right*: Trooper George Plafcan with items from the Mountain Man case, now in the PA State Police museum. *Photo by Blair Shore, courtesy of Sandy Kleckner. Right*: Marie Henry, RN with Peggy in the hospital, May 1966. *Collection of P. Jackson*

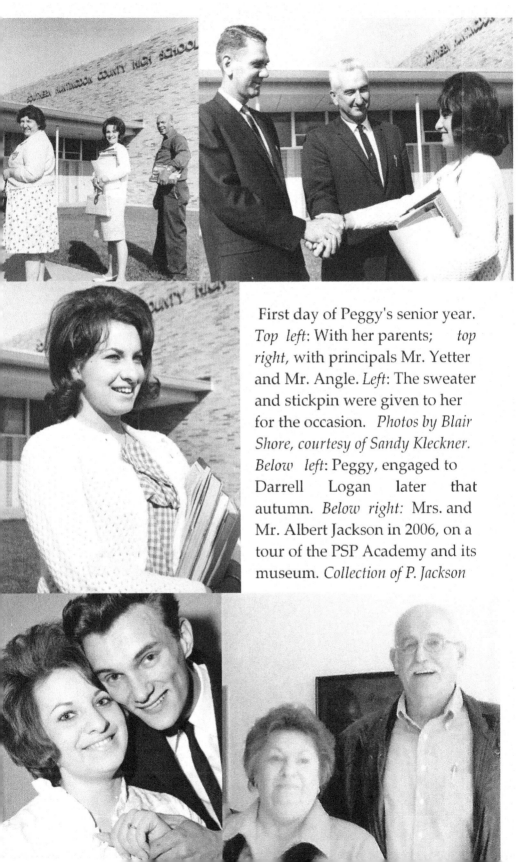

First day of Peggy's senior year. *Top left*: With her parents; *top right*, with principals Mr. Yetter and Mr. Angle. *Left*: The sweater and stickpin were given to her for the occasion. *Photos by Blair Shore, courtesy of Sandy Kleckner. Below left*: Peggy, engaged to Darrell Logan later that autumn. *Below right:* Mrs. and Mr. Albert Jackson in 2006, on a tour of the PSP Academy and its museum. *Collection of P. Jackson*

Scrapbook

SAFE AT LAST. Peggy Bradnick weari[ng] leans against her rescuers as she is led fro[m] the Rubeck farmyard.

THE DAILY NEWS

1966, Peggy Ann kidnapping

40 years later, much has changed; details still remain fresh

E JUNIATA   SATURDAY, MAY 27, 2006 Section A — Page 11

Classmates Greet Peggy Ann At Southern

It's been 40 years since the kidnapping of Peggy Ann Bradnick, 17, of the Shade Gap area. Peggy is now Mrs. Albert Jackson of Three Springs and has come a long way from the days at Southern Huntingdon County High School. Julia (Duvall) Lemin of Cedar Crest, Mount Union, remembers those days and visited The Daily News this week with this clipping from the June 2, 1966, edition of The Daily News she saved. That's Peggy Bradnick at the left after she returned to school. Greeting her were Kathy Pheasant (now of California), Julia Duvall, Devina Russell, now Abrashoff, and Patsy Pollock, now Sipes. Devina is the owner of Sophie's Beauty Shop in Mount Union and Patsy and her husband have an animal-raising farm near Mount Union. Julia said she remembered that Peggy was wearing her red corduroy jumper and a white blouse on the day she was abducted by William Hollenbaugh (May 11, 1966). All the girls were wearing outfits they made in home ec class for the photo. Julia said. The older boys were excused from classes to help search for Peggy and the girls were "all scared." She remembers being grateful that it had ended and Peggy was safe.

STANDING WATCH. Thomas Shelar, an off-duty trooper, boosts himself on milk cans to scan the hills.

GOD INSPIRES I[T]

Peggy Ann Bradnick Jackson marks 50t[h] anniversary of kidnapping near Shade Ga[p]

ON THE SCENT. Specially trained dogs [lead] four state policemen across a meadow belo[w] the piney Tuscarora range on the trail of the kidnaper. Helicopters were used in the sea[rch]

I've heard from a few people who worked or hunted with Hollenbaugh that he was very intelligent in his way. But all I can think ever since when I see his picture is that he was pure evil.

[Hollenbaugh did brag about shooting Ned Price to Peggy. There has never been any solid reason to question his statement. Later reports of someone shooting at cars on the Turnpike may have fallen within Hollenbaugh's timeframe, but without comment from the press.]

Marie Henry, RN (retired)

[Transcript of a handwritten statement kindly made for Peggy by Mrs. Henry, who at nearly ninety-five years of age is sound of body and mind, and very active.]

In 1966 I was an RN in at the Fulton County Medical Center, McConnellsburg, Pa. We were a small hospital but we had everything. We had patients, emergencies, deliveries and surgery. We had 1 nurse, 3 doctors – Dr. McLucas, Dr. Lorenz and Dr. Fry. We had aides, orderlies, & some LPN's and an X-Ray nurse on, Wayne Lake, who was also our all-around man. We were like one happy family. We helped each other. I loved it.

Sometimes we had 2 RN's on. Mostly weekends. Most of them only wanted to work 2 days a week. Mostly weekends were really busy. We had all kinds of emergencies from our two mountains, Tuscarora, & Sideling Hill, and the Pa Turnpike. Even our office people were friends & [so were the] kitchen people. The night before Peggy was rescued I worked 3 to 11 shift. Mrs. Palmer, our nurse supervisor, called me and said she couldn't come to work the next day, could I come back in. I told her I would. So I got home and came back in at 7a.m. That was when everything broke loose. Peggy was rescued and the Mountain Man was shot and killed.

Peggy was brought in by Fire Company ambulance, and the Mountain Man. [*N.B.: This is the only detail with which Peggy disagrees. She was brought in a marked State Police cruiser, sitting in the back seat, in the company of FBI Agents Briner and O'Connor, while Hollenbaugh was brought in by ambulance a little while after her.*]

Peggy was exhausted, scared and hungry. If I remember right she had a pair of his pants and boots on. We removed them, gave her a good bath & washed her hair. Then we gave her a good meal.

She was examined by the doctor and we gave her something to calm and relax her. Then the F.B.I. questioned her. I stayed with her the whole time. Then the news reporters got their news about it.

In the meantime Kelso's Funeral Home came and took his [Hollenbaugh's] body out. I have a newspaper picture of that. Jack Kelso and Harry Reeder got the body. I am in the picture, and an aide and X-Ray man, Wayne.

I know the Lord was with Peggy. He never left or forsook her. Like me, he never leaves or forsakes me. Peggy was so excited to see her Mom, Dad, sisters and brothers as well as they were. Each day Peggy became stronger and happier. She was allowed up out of bed. Peggy made a lot of friends with the patients and they with her. That made her spirits better. I didn't see Peggy again until she was grown. One day my friend Sarah Smith who was an L.P.N. at the hospital had a big yard sale. I was there and Peggy came to it. Sarah invited Peggy and I back that week to lunch and she brought a pie if I can remember and I don't remember what Sarah & I made. But we enjoyed our lunch and had a wonderful day.

I did not see Peggy again until when she was in at the Central Fulton School in

McC[onnells]b[ur]g to speak. My daughter and I went. I had my picture taken with her. I have a picture taken with her in the hospital 50 years ago. Then I saw her again in 2016 April 16. The Historical Society had her up at the dinner at Hustontown Fire Hall. She was glad to see me. I had my picture taken with her then. I am so happy she has God in her life & heart, as I have Him in mine. God loves us all.

Jean McMullen

We used to see Bicycle Pete around a lot, riding his red bike with that little dog in the basket, but I never got a good look at his face.

Growing up, my cousin Peggy and I – our fathers were brothers – were good friends, and I remember us doing each other's hair. By the time she was in high school I was married and had two boys.

During the years we were dealing with the Mountain Man, we were on our guard, but we had our lives to live and couldn't spare the time to cower behind closed doors or anything.

One summer evening around dusk I was

taking out trash. My youngest was in the playpen, and my older boy had followed me out onto the porch, as always; he followed me everywhere. When I reached the steps, a hand grabbed my ankle. I yelled and broke free. A man hiding under the porch stairs had grabbed me, and when I got loose he came out and I got a look at him – his face was covered and he was wearing a raincoat. Of course I ran inside with the boys, and waited for my husband to return.

I didn't connect the man I saw with Bicycle Pete at the time, but when he was identified as the Mountain Man I was prepared to swear it was him who had tried to grab me. Until after he took Peggy I'd never heard his real name.

I never expected to see her alive again, when I heard she'd been kidnapped; and when I heard what she'd been through, I was sure I'd never have been able to survive as she did. I'd have done something wrong and been killed.

Sharon Querry

On Thursday, June 25, 1964, my father went to open his store, A.R. Houck's Hardware in

Orbisonia, and found that it had been broken into during the night. There were portable transistor radios missing, and watches, and loose change, but what concerned Dad the most was the two guns, by far the most expensive items. One was a pump-action 12-gauge shotgun, the other was a Winchester Model 94 .30-.30. He never got either of them back, and it was two years before we even found out anything. Dad identified the sawed-off shotgun used by the Mountain Man to kill the FBI agent as the one taken from his store that night; likewise, the Philco radio in its case. Dad wanted the shotgun back, but sawed-off shotguns are illegal, and the State Police kept it. The .30-.30 was never recovered that I ever heard. I don't remember what else might have been stolen that night, whether ammunition or batteries or any other small items. I can't say how Bicycle Pete, as he was called, took that much stuff with him, whether on foot or on his bicycle.

Three other businesses were burglarized that night – another hardware store, the bank, and the custard stand north of town, but not as much went missing from those places, and nothing at all was taken from the bank.

One evening it was getting dark when we

saw a man watching our house in Orbisonia; he was dressed in an overcoat. Mom closed the curtains and we waited for Dad to come home. He dismissed the incident, but I found out later that he hadn't wanted us to worry. The stranger had gone the other way when Dad came up to the house, and he was sure it was the Mountain Man, especially since the store was broken into.

A few months after he was killed, the State Police announced that they were satisfied that Hollenbaugh had committed all four burglaries that night in 1964.

I knew Peggy from school, and then we went to beauty school together. I remember that her legs had purple scars showing for as long as we were there, because of course girls had to wear knee-length skirts at the time.

I have to ask, what if William Hollenbaugh hadn't been so set upon being a criminal? What might he have contributed to society? For example, he'd done other things to that shotgun, not just shortening the barrel and chiseling out the serial number. Anyone bright enough to do what he did is a loss.

Alicia Marie Logan

[From a statement written expressly for Peggy and this book]

I am often asked what it was like, growing up the only child of a kidnap victim. The first thing I do is correct the individual that my mom, Peggy Ann, is not a victim but a survivor. "Victim" is a proper description in that she was harmed and injured as a result of a crime, but it does not define her. Being a survivor allows her the opportunity to still see the good in people, especially those who gave their time, and one who made the ultimate sacrifice with his life.

I did not know of the kidnapping until I accidentally came across the *LIFE** magazine interview, initially thinking it [the cover] came from a carnival photo booth. I questioned why Daddy wasn't in the picture too. I vividly remember that day. Mom laughed and said, "Bring that here and sit on the couch with me so we can take a look at it together." We sat on the big gold-covered couch that was made especially for my 6-foot-2-inch Dad to be able to stretch out on, and she opened the zipper bag and took out the magazine. Then I realized it was a *real* magazine. Mom said, "There is a story inside. I want you to read it, and I will help you with any words you don't know. Then we can talk about the story that really happened to me." We sat for a long time while I read the article and looked at the pictures of my Grandparents, and my Aunts and Uncles when they were much smaller. Mom was insistent that although bad things happen, we must still enjoy life and all of the good things we can do.

After learning of the kidnapping, not much changed for me. I still went on field trips in school, sleepovers, band trips, and basically all the things an elementary and junior high school girl does. Education was a big thing in our house, even after my Dad died of cancer. I went back to school [in Indiana] the week after he was buried in Pennsylvania, determined to get my diploma and make them both proud. Dad had graduated and was able to attend all of the customary traditions like walking across the stage. Mom wasn't able to do that [ceremony] so I wanted to make sure she was able to be a part of the graduation tradition by seeing me graduate.

After getting married and having my son, then ultimately getting a divorce, we – Mom had remarried and Al, *aka* Dad – decided it was time for a change. We moved from the state of Indiana back to Pennsylvania near my Grandma and my Aunts and Uncles. During this time Mom was often asked questions about the kidnapping and [about] several of the rumors that still surround the event. She chose to begin doing public speaking engagements to help those who have suffered tragedies know that life can still be good, and that the first thing you need to do every day that God gives you is to thank Him that you have that day, because tomorrow is not a guarantee.

I, however, would prefer to remain out of the public eye. I enjoy my quiet life raising my Shih Tzu's and, unfortunately, dealing with my own health issues. I do get on the blogs occasionally to dispel rumors about my paternity or about my Mom's participation in other books that have been written about her kidnapping.

I am taken aback at the overwhelming response she has received as she traveled throughout the state, meeting people who helped look for her and those who cared for her in the hospital, that still are so warm and giving. I am very appreciative to all of those who continue to serve the community and help their neighbors as they did all those years ago when a teenage girl was taken from the school bus stop in the middle of the woods. We need to return to those days when friendship was more important than material possessions and a hug wasn't a bad thing. In my opinion people would be so much happier and less stressed if they just allowed themselves to put their faith in whatever god they choose and lend a hand and a smile to those they meet. In doing so, we can all be survivors.

---

*NB: The Saturday Evening Post of July 16, 1966 was the magazine that carried a picture of Peggy on its cover. LIFE Magazine had a different cover story when they ran their article on the kidnapping.

Chapter 9

There are a few questions that people always ask me: was there any sexual assault during my abduction (no), and who really shot Hollenbaugh (Trooper Mixell, according to the coroner's report, but people still argue about that.) But the big question is, what has happened since? Right now, that covers fifty years.

I won't include much, but there are a few things I feel are important. Like anyone else, a full account of my life would take many boring volumes, rather than a few chapters.

I started cosmetology classes in Lewistown soon after I was released from the hospital. They began by asking what I did for makeup, so I told them: plain water and cold cream on the face; eyebrow pencil, or ordinary school graphite pencil if the proper sort wasn't available. Lipstick from the samples my aunt saved for us, with a bobby pin to scrape out every last bit from the bottom. My colors tend to be lighter pinks and the colors we had for free were often much darker, so Mom taught me how to dilute them with petroleum jelly. My complexion didn't require base, and for rouge we dabbed a bit of lipstick off our lips and rubbed it over our cheekbones, so the colors always matched.

I received some blank looks, but they taught me anyway.

Before my senior year started, friends invited my family to a summer picnic up in Strodes Mills. The important thing about that day was that I met Darrell Logan. His sisters had pointed me out to him, but he didn't know why they thought I was notable until I told him about the kidnapping; he thought maybe I'd been in an accident. He never took time to read the papers.

Darrell was a hard-working man, the eminently employable sort. As soon as it was legal for him to work, he did. Before he was out of school he was managing Dank's in Lewistown and Poser's in Huntingdon, two clothing stores. He went on to a trucking company, first on the docks and later as a driver. He did all this despite his health, which was never good.

To make a short story shorter, Dad must have figured that I could take care of myself around a boyfriend, and raised no objection to Darrell dating me. We saw each other when we had time; it was never a great romantic affair. We were married within a year of our meeting, on his grandmother's birthday, March 23rd, 1967, at the Pleasant Hill church I'd attended for years.

I thought that next morning that I'd cook my new husband breakfast. The eggs and toast were just done when there was a knock at the door. Two reporters had come all the way to Lewistown from Pittsburgh to check on how Peggy Ann Bradnick's honeymoon was going, and literally got a foot in the door before I could close it. I told them to leave, but they tried to get their questions in anyway.

"Didn't you hear my wife?" said Darrell right behind me, backing me up. "As of yesterday, she no longer answers to Bradnick." After a few more minutes they left, unsatisfied. Then, instead of the hot breakfast I'd wanted to serve, we shared cold egg sandwiches.

He had to go in to work for a while that day. When he left, I sat on the bed and cried.

The next day he was in the hospital to have kidney stones removed. It was Easter weekend.

In Dad's world, girls didn't have to know how to drive. Mom knew how and had taken over from Dad when he was drunk, but never got her license. Darrell, on the other hand, insisted that I learn: how was I to get around while he was at work if I didn't? When we bought the mobile home that was our first house, I had money to put on it. He put it in my name. It was a revolutionary experience, being married to a fair-minded man.

I was one of several girls in my class to graduate after marriage, but what with one thing and another – the thirty-mile drive one way from Strodes Mills, concentrating on my cosmetology classes that week, and avoiding the public eye – I didn't attend the commencement ceremony.

Our daughter was born later that year, after a very difficult pregnancy. I had very little time with my tiny newborn before I went in to surgery to stop the bleeding. I was unable afterward to have any more children.

Dad had wanted to name me Margaret

when I was born, but Mom had refused to saddle a cute baby with an "old-lady" name, so "Peggy" is now the full given name of a retired grandmother. Darrell and I avoided that situation for our child, naming her Alicia. Thanks to him, the press got no pictures of us when she was born, but not because they didn't want to.

We had been married over a year when Darrell's company transferred him out to Indiana, and we settled in a trailer park in Westville until we bought a house. I was surprised at the number of Pennsylvania expatriates I met in the Valparaiso area, many of whom knew or were from Huntingdon County.

There were challenges there. I didn't suffer from agoraphobia even after a lifetime in the mountains, but the air felt stale at first and the endless flat cornfields were disorienting. On Darrell's first day of work, he advised that the best way to find what we needed was to go out and look for it; so I took off in the car with the baby, picking a direction at random. After exploring awhile, noting stores and such, I ended up in Valparaiso and saw a familiar truck at a depot. "You found me," grinned my husband.

Those were the best years of our marriage.

Alicia and I accompanied Darrell when we could, traveling all over the country until we'd been in all of the lower forty- eight states. We had to stop when Alicia was old enough for preschool and then school, and Darrell went out by himself while I took care of her. After a few days of our child being at school all day, I got bored and found a job.

It was the time of moon shots, Vietnam, and eventually Watergate. Hurricane Agnes and the Flood of 1972 didn't affect us out in Indiana at all, except for worrying about our families. The Vietnam War ended. OPEC cut oil supplies, raising fuel prices drastically; in 1974 came the Teamsters' strike that stranded Darrell in Corpus Christi for a week or so, and then came the nation's Bicentennial. Personally, that was a relief. The tenth year after the abduction might have drawn more unwanted attention if not for that yearlong-plus celebration.

By that time, my brothers and sisters had begun to leave school and move away. Mary's senior trip had been to Washington, DC. They took in the FBI Museum, and she nearly fainted when she saw my red corduroy dress on display. How it had gotten there from the hospital floor I don't know.

All three of my sisters learned to drive. The age gap between James and Mary meant that Mom and Dad essentially raised two batches of kids, and the younger siblings had very different high school years than I'd had.

To the last, Grandma Goldie Bradnick enjoyed a healthy onion sandwich before bed. She passed away quietly one evening in 1973, in her favorite chair with an onion sandwich at her side, watching her beloved *Hee Haw*.

Darrell and I had never told our daughter about the kidnapping. We didn't want her to grow up afraid. Alicia remembers the circumstances somewhat differently, but what I recall is that one day when she was in second grade, Alicia came home miffed.

"Mommy, the girl behind me said mean things about you! She said you were famous."

Uh-oh. I knew who Alicia meant; the girl's grandmother must have figured out who I was.

"She said you were adducted!"

"What?"

"She said you were kidnapped, what's the word...."

"Abducted?"

"Yeah."

I'd wanted to wait until she was older, but now I could bring out the magazines and things and at least explain the event on my terms. Alicia took it in, and has never really asked much about it since. My daughter did tell the girl sitting behind her in school that yes, it had happened, but also that she was proud that I was her mom.

Alicia was still in grade school when we took a wrong turn.

Darrell worked hard to provide for his family, and we saw him less and less. Alicia barely knew him. The only vacation we ever took was to have been a few days at the ocean, stopping in to see our families on the way back; but Darrell fretted so much about not working that we left after sixteen hours. He suffered from migraines, and when taken to the hospital he would worry about all we'd have to go without because of missing a day's pay – although we could well afford days off by then.

When he was offered a management position, both of us thought that it would mean a better life – more money, and also less road time with more family time.

We were wrong.

The switch from blue collar to white meant immersion in a wholly unfamiliar culture. We acquired a bigger house with a big mortgage in a good neighborhood, which I kept up while working myself. There were dinners and visitors, sometimes at very short notice, at other houses or at ours, with a whole new set of people who were to be impressed rather than befriended.

I'd always dressed well. "I love you, honey, but you're not going to school like that" was how Mom put it when she inspected each of us before we boarded the bus every morning. That ingrained principle of always being presentable worked for me now, especially since I'd never liked shopping for clothes. Likewise, I had always been able to cook and to socialize.

This, though, was different. In this circle, I was one of maybe half a dozen wives of CEO's and CFO's and the like, and it seemed as if it were every woman for herself. I wasn't sure of their backgrounds, but they ranged from one wife who didn't work, to the lady I knew least but might have wanted to know better, who was a nurse. All I knew of her was that she had been raised on a farm and her hours seldom permitted her to attend parties. I remember her husband as one of the sort who was amazed that other people could afford anything like he had, down to a paddleball "desktop stress-reduction aid" such as we'd given out for favors at Alicia's birthday party.

I remember once describing a dinner menu to one of the women. "You'll use a chafing dish for the sauce, of course," she said. Not, for instance, "Do you have one? I can lend you mine." But by this time I had learned a bit.

"Of course," I replied, not batting an eye. "Wouldn't you?"

Then I went out and found out what a chafing dish was and how to use one. My usual source was stores. This time I ended up at an event-supply business that rented less-common necessities for weddings and so on.

"Do you just need to rent one, or are you interested in buying?" asked the very helpful and informative saleslady. They had used ones for sale. I bought one I liked for two dollars, and the sauce turned out just as well as if I'd used, say, the double boiler.

I had a few rules for our house, one of which was BYOB. I would not provide alcohol; I'd had too much experience with it. Another thing I refused to give up was putting Alicia to bed myself, no matter who came to dinner. It distanced me from the crowd a little more.

Darrell threw himself into the new life with enthusiasm. It had all the challenge he wanted, and more. His father had been a hard man, sending his children out to work as soon as they were able. Darrell was making it big with that ethic behind him, but the American Dream was much more a nightmare for us. A few times, he questioned whether what he was doing was right; but never to the point of giving up the job. Darrell was loyal to his employers to a fault.

That job took up even more of his time than truck driving. There was work, and travel, and keeping up the right society. He began to drink socially, at other houses or at restaurants like *The Orange Bowl*, a place to dine and be seen.

There was more expected of a man in his position. One day he came home with a *boat*. What about a place for it on the lake, and the insurance, and maintenance – and, I didn't say aloud, the mortgage we were trying to pay off...?

"All taken care of," he said, smiling. That weekend I was going out of town to visit some of his family in Ohio, and my sister Carol Jean was stopping by our house, so she actually knew more about the thing than I did.

There was a great difference between Darrell and the men he worked with, though, who had always had boats of their own on Lake Michigan. Darrel could not only operate one, he could maintain and fix it too.

Still, we saw very little of each other, and when he was home I found him changed. More and more he was buying into this new life, while I was trying to keep myself and my daughter separate from an existence I felt was almost wholly superficial. A great deal more began to intrude, and about a year later I'd had enough. Alicia shouldn't be raised in such an atmosphere. I arranged for a dinner at *The Orange Bowl*.

"I've filed for divorce," I told him. Divorce was a bigger deal then, much bigger for a woman professing to be a Christian, but there were too many good reasons by that time.

His only comment was, "Are you going to keep Alicia away from me?"

"No, of course not. She's your daughter."

It didn't happen that way, though. Soon after that meeting, before the lawyers could move, he fell sick. Afterward, he finally quit that job and went back to trucking. He had a physical before being allowed back out on the road. He'd been driving about six weeks that summer when the news came back about a lump they'd found under his collarbone: it was cancer.

I stopped the proceedings; what was the use? I could have let him go to his brother in Ohio, who could afford to take care of an invalid, but no. He was still my husband. He had to go on medical leave and shortly became bedridden.

I cared for him and ferried the doctors' reports to his supervisors, and eventually had to take time off from my own job. My employers were wonderful. They told me not to worry. The Kingsburys were a couple who had a butchering business that supplied restaurants and caterers as well as retail shoppers. I'd worked my way up to manager, despite knowing little about butchering when I was hired. But when I had to stop working, they gave me leave at full pay, and would bring by a box of meat now and again.

The rest of the neighborhood was like that, too. When Darrell could no longer eat solid food, moving to frozen fudge pops, the grocer across the street would call Alicia over and give her a box of them daily. The area was booming, and the businesses believed in passing on their blessings. One place held a fundraiser, and the owner brought by a bag with five thousand dollars in all denominations from pennies on up.

In that last illness, Darrell asked and was given my forgiveness. We had both been at fault, but the rest had to be between himself and God. Almost the last thing he said was that his only regret was that he couldn't go back to work. He had no idea what pain that caused.

Darrell Logan passed away on February 19, 1980. Of all those he had worked for and socialized with, only his boss showed up; and he let slip that he was obliged to be there. But the press came.

I took Darrell home to be buried near Lewistown. It was expensive. When Alicia and I returned to Indiana, I had to hire a lawyer to get Darrell's benefits. Despite all the loyalty and labor he had given to the trucking company since his teens, despite all the documentation of his illness, they tried to claim that he had quit voluntarily and deserved nothing from them.

I was left a widow at twenty-nine, a single mother with a mortgage and with no family nearby, alone and very much afraid.

Chapter 10

Fear could not be allowed to rule my life. I had a child to raise. I will always call my marriage to Darrell a good one, but whatever a young widow should feel, whatever grief and loss, was almost entirely missing – leached out of the relationship by long absence and overwork.

I went back to work after the funeral. In addition to managing the butcher shop, I added a second and then a third job. The Kingsburys always encouraged me to have anything I needed from the cooler, and it was a great help. Slowly, so slowly, I paid off the debt as I kept up with the bills.

After the house was paid for I quit two of

the jobs. My daughter shouldn't have everything handed to her, I thought, and I was tired.

For the record, while I was struggling with all that, Darrell's old company fell on hard times. He'd always said that the place could be run by only five people. I don't know how many careers survived among the company's elite with which we once mingled. I felt that they had looked upon a young widow as a threat to their marriages (because of course I'd be prowling for a new husband, how could I live otherwise, where else would I possibly look, etc. etc.) Meanwhile, I set out to earn enough money to keep a house.

Alicia was able to do a lot of things in and out of school that I had never dreamed of doing: sports, music, drama, speech and debate, a modeling class – and I was able to discover them for the first time along with her. My only stipulation was that whatever she did, she had to follow through. No quitting halfway through the season or semester, no letting her teammates down. But after that, I wouldn't insist that she pursue anything she didn't want to.

The modeling class was a good example. Physically, Alicia was right for it. The teacher impressed me as well. She made sure her students knew the unvarnished truth about the profession, as well as letting the parents observe class anytime they wanted to. Alicia decided not to pursue it as a career after that, rightly I think, and I considered the fee money well spent.

Eventually she became an accountant.

When she was sixteen I happily signed a permission slip for her to work after school at a hamburger joint, not so much for the sixty-odd dollars on each paycheck as for the experience.

I would have been content to spend the rest of my life like that. The Kingsburys seemed to be grooming me to take over the business, my daughter was my best friend and I was raising her as well as I could in the nice house that Darrell had left us and that I was steadily paying off. My family came out to visit in bits and pieces and we went back to Pennsylvania now and again. I had gotten involved with the local emergency services, ran with the ambulance, and hosted their meetings at home. I had made some real friends.

God had other plans.

While I was still working to pay off the house, Mary came out for a visit. Her boyfriend at the time was a trucker whose company was based in the area, and she rode out to Indiana with him and a friend of his. All three stopped at the house when they arrived that evening. Mary chided me for rudeness; I'd done no more than greet the men briefly.

"I don't mean to be rude," I said wearily. "It's just that it's been a long day and I have to be up at five-thirty in the morning."

I made a little more time that evening. Mary brought them by again after that. The boyfriend didn't make any deep impression on me, nor indeed upon Mary. His friend Albert, though, I didn't like at all. He was too perfect, seemingly entirely honest and up-front to the point that he couldn't be genuine. That he was tall and handsome as well didn't reassure me. He didn't seem to have any faults; I'm not counting his wicked sense of humor. For some reason, he seemed to want me to change, one way or another, and I had no attention to spare for that; I was fine as I was, end of story, just busy.

It took a long time to trust him, but it happened. I met his family, who were farmers from Wisconsin. His brothers and sisters were all as laid-back as he was, not interfering with one another at all to the point that I wondered how such a family could possibly function.

Things progressed. Al and Alicia got along well. My family liked him too, and when we went to Pennsylvania I introduced him to Darrell's family, who approved of him. We visited Darrell's grave too while we were there.

I passed a test posed by his sister: she had me meet a mare of hers. I had no experience with horses to speak of, aside from riding in a buckboard behind Mrs. Kelly's Gypsy a few times in first grade. I approached this one in her pasture, fed her the apple I'd been given without losing my hand and scratched her neck as she sniffed me up and down and asked for more attention. It seems to have been the right thing to do, because Al's sister approved me for inclusion in their circle.

Sometimes you have a grand romance or plans for the future, and sometimes you marry your best friend, for no other reason than that you want to. On October 1st of 1983 Albert Jackson and I were married.

From the beginning, Al had a gift that my first husband had lacked – that of making the three of us into a real family. Alicia has always looked to him as her real father.

My mother summed it all up: "Most women

don't have one good marriage," she told me one day. "You've had two." It still holds true.

The miserable year and more we'd spent in higher society was now a long time ago. I had no idea how much it still had hold of me.

Among our neighbors was a couple from Pennsylvania with their son. Sad to say, the boy spent a lot of time with us rather than with his parents, but we were as good to him as we could be. Kevin was younger than Alicia, who treated him like a little brother.

There were nights when we'd hear someone at the door. One of us would go downstairs and he'd be there, asking if he could stay with us. We'd let him stay, locking the door and reassuring him that no one could get in. His parents never came looking for him.

Kevin was very anxious that year that I should come to his last baseball game of the season. I promised, and had every intention of going.

Al came in on the afternoon. My hair was still up and I wasn't dressed to go out. "What are you doing?" he asked. "Aren't you supposed to be at the game?"

I'd completely forgotten. I deflated; there was no way I'd be ready before the game was over now. "I can't go like this!" I mourned.

"But you can disappoint that boy? Come on," he ordered, picking up the keys. "We're going."

"But my hair isn't ready, and I'm not dressed – "

"Throw on anything! Put a scarf over your hair! No one will care."

I did. Five minutes later, feeling as conspicuous as if I were still in pajamas, we left the house.

Al, bless him, was absolutely right. No one paid a bit of attention to how I was dressed or that my hair wasn't done under the scarf. They paid attention to the game. The only one who looked at me was Kevin, who grinned his biggest grin at seeing us there.

I haven't completely let myself go since then, of course. But I've never forgotten that I really don't have to feel as if I perpetually live in a fishbowl anymore.

I can be proud of our boy, too. Kevin is now a doctor.

There were other things that happened

while we lived in Indiana. Once I was caught in a dust storm and stranded along the highway for twenty-four hours. Four times I've seen tornados, and have one piece of advice: Heed the warnings, immediately. They happen fast.

The closest call came around the beginning of May in 1987. Our house was in the small town of Hamlet, near Route 30. I was home that day, looking after my brand-new grandson Brian while Alicia was at work. It looked ugly outside, so I watched the TV for the weather. I'd just seen the warning when I heard the sirens go off: Knox, Kingsbury, LaPorte – I realized that it must be heading for us. Quickly I slid the napping Brian under the heavy bed and joined him –

WHOOM

The door slammed. "Mom! Mom, are you all right?"

We were. That fast, the twister skipped over our side of the street and the storm went on to wreak havoc in a trailer park in Warsaw, a few miles away. I slid the baby out from under the bed and put him back in the bassinet. He'd slept through the whole thing.

We were still cleaning up debris and tree branches later that week when Mary and her husband Terry arrived for a visit. The actual damage to our house consisted of a missing pool cover and a gutter torn loose.

In 1967, it was only a matter of months after I married Darrell that my parents moved again, this time to a house across the road from the Shade Gap Elementary School, where Mom had found work. After that they moved to a trailer park in Orbisonia, but Mom stayed with the job at the school and never went back to the cannery again. She'd babysit Alicia there in Shade Gap while I was in Lewistown practicing for my beautician's license.

The most visible and profound change from the events surrounding my abduction may have been in my father. While I was forging ahead with my life, so was he. He was hired by an agency, and worked as the night watchman at the heavy equipment factory in McConnellsburg until he retired. It was a job no one else wanted, but Dad was fearless and never had a problem there that he couldn't handle.

The one thing that never changed was the frequent moving. Even after it was no longer necessary, Dad was too restless stay in one house too long. He would simply come home one day, saying that he'd seen a place for rent, and he thought they'd be better off there. Soon after, there would be another move.

Because of what he'd put us through all those years, after he sobered up he always felt a great understanding and compassion toward alcoholics and the inebriated. He also gained a reputation as a bouncer. He discovered an ability to talk down the rowdiest of drunks at events like the Shade Gap Picnic. If they couldn't be talked down and things got physical, Dad could handle that too, thanks to what he'd learned in the Army.

Grandma Goldie's house stood vacant for some years after the estate was settled. Eventually my uncle, the executor, allowed Dad and Mom to live there for a while, although it was just two rooms and an attic. I knew they were in the process of moving out a few years later when my phone rang one night in Indiana.

"Someone torched the house," Dad said shortly. No one was hurt, and what my parents lost amounted to some of the furniture, not much of value. He suspected that a neighbor's son, maybe with some other friends, had broken in and set the fire after they'd partied. It was an old wooden building and had gone up too quickly for the fire department to arrive. Fortunately, the fire hadn't spread to the other sheds nearby.

There had been other losses, though. Practically all the memorabilia from after I'd been rescued had been stored in the attic and was gone – the dress from the President and First Lady, the cards and letters I'd kept from all over the world, the servicemen's medals, even Grandma Goldie's Bible with the statement I'd written for that TV interview tucked inside.

I was sorry, but not devastated. There was too much else going on in my life at the time for me to mourn the destruction. Still, it might have made a museum or historical society happy one day.

Despite the lack of insurance, Dad never pursued the crime. He figured it wasn't worth ruining a kid's life and a father's friendship.

My siblings remembered what things had been like during Dad's drunken rages, but had been given the chance to experience life without them. I barely knew such a time, since I'd moved out when I did, and I'd gone through more years of his temper. My feelings about it all came to a head during a visit home.

We were by ourselves in the car, and I asked him to pull over for a moment.

"What's up?" he wondered.

I let him know. I told him about the anger I'd harbored for decades, over the way he'd treated all of us but most especially Mom for the first seventeen years I'd known them.

"What do you want me to do?" he asked me somberly when I'd finished.

"Give your life to God," I urged him. We spoke some more; but at the end all he said was, "I'll think about it."

I suppose that was the most I could expect of Dad or anyone else, since everyone's soul is between that person and God.

When I spent those two weeks in the Fulton County Medical Center, my room hadn't smelled like a hospital. It had smelled strongly of coffee. To make it smell like home, though, would have required aromas from dinner on the stove and smoke from Dad's Camels. He'd smoked from a very early age – eight or nine years old.

I'd been married to Al for a few years when my sister Carol Jean brought Mom and Dad out to

Indiana for a visit. They were almost to the house when Dad wanted to stop at a florist shop to get me a bouquet.

He'd never done anything like that for me. Carol Jean dropped a word in the ear of the attendant that it was for me; the shop was one of the places I'd worked. They sold Dad a huge and beautiful collection of day-old flowers, enough that I had to scramble to get them all in whatever would hold water. Normally the flowers should have lasted for a few days at most. These lasted for two weeks, with a change of water every few days.

But like my sister, I knew this wasn't characteristic of my Dad. It drove home the knowledge that he must be sick, very sick.

He was. He was dying of lung cancer.

Dad had said that he would think about giving his life to God, and he was a man of his word: he thought about it, and entrusted himself to the Lord on December 20, 1987, while in the hospital. Three days later, we knew he didn't have much longer. Dad told Mom that what he really wanted right then was a final cigarette. Mom thought about it for a moment, then turned off the oxygen and lit one for him. A doctor smelled the smoke from down the hall. "What are you *doing*?" he demanded from the doorway.

"Last rites," replied Mom succinctly. The doctor took in the turned-off oxygen and the dying man in the bed, and realized that it was pretty late to expect Dad to benefit from kicking the habit. He left without saying more.

On the day before Christmas Eve, Gene Bradnick passed away.

After Dad died, Mom lived alone in Orbisonia, although most of us lived fairly close. A few years later Al was ready to move away from the Midwest. We decided to move back to Pennsylvania. Before we could do that, though, something unusual turned up: I found out that Hollywood had come calling, in the most impolite manner.

Chapter 11

"Mom, I've known you all my life. I know you hide things from me. What is it?" Visiting my mother, I had been shocked to see her in tears after several phone calls one afternoon.

After some prying, it came out. For over two decades, ever since the kidnapping, my parents had been harassed by movie producers and writers. They had never let on about it to me.

"I'll pay for the call," I promised, and dialed the number the caller had given. After a mutual exchange of distrust in each other's identity and intention, I got to the point.

"I'm going to say this once. This is my lawyer's number. I will be talking to him. I expect you to call within the next day."

The long process initiated that afternoon resulted in a made-for-television movie, after many months and sixteen revisions, and nearly getting sued by the producers for the delays. The result fulfilled my conditions that it stick as closely as possible to the course of events, that it treat the subject matter and the people in the story with respect, and that it be family-friendly enough to show in schools.

It was far from a documentary, however. If I'd thought they really would do the story justice, I wouldn't have gotten involved. It was, first and foremost, *entertainment*; that was in the contract I signed, from the beginning. There was absolutely no way that the complexity of the actual events, with the thousands of participants and residents and the landscape and everything else, could possibly make it to a TV screen in the time given. I had an idea that no matter how hard the production company tried (if they did try) no one involved in the original events would like the result anyway – especially after I'd read through the first draft of the script.

Where, I wondered, could anyone get such ideas about what had taken place?

So, I specified certain conditions. It wasn't to be made here around Shade Gap; unless they filmed in late April and early May it would never be accurate anyway, and there would probably be an army of helpful neighbors showing up to tell the crew where they were getting it wrong. I didn't provide any photos of anyone involved. I had to approve the script, per the contract my lawyer and I had come up with, but I understood that I had to leave them a *story* rather than a history.

For the record, the title is *Cry in the Wild: The Taking of Peggy Ann.* It was written by Durrel Royce Crays and produced by Leonard Hill Films and Criss Cross Productions, directed by Charles Correl, and starred Megan Follows, David Soul, David Morse, and a host of others speaking in an accent that came from a long way south of Huntingdon County. Over the course of a few hours (including ads) as much truth and history slipped in as the writer and I could manage. Inaccurate things happened to a few characters who took on the roles of dozens of people, amid a hail of inaccurate gunfire. In a word, Hollywood happened.

As expected, it wasn't well reviewed by the

people who lived through that time. One of the State Troopers involved declared that he ought to write a book about what had really taken place. He should have; I wish he had.

The only member of the production team that I met was Durrel Crays, who came to Shade Gap. I was never invited to the set or anything. I'd cost them enough already, I guess. I'm sure I would have found it interesting and amusing.

The first script was done before I became involved and was, in my opinion, trashy. To put it bluntly, where had love or sex ever come into it? If that was what the kidnapper had wanted, my only defense would have been to fight until I was shot, and Hollenbaugh had been strong enough that there was no guarantee that I could have physically resisted him. Where had that even come from?

That turned out to be a more intriguing question than I'd ever realized.

The script writer gave me a document he'd acquired during his research. That copy now has my comments in the margins: "No," "Never happened," "Never said that" and the like. I gave up in disgust after a few pages. It was disturbingly twisted and ridiculous.

But for years afterward a question bothered me: *where had it come from?* Was this the State Police and FBI transcribing what I had told them in an interview that happened Thursday May 19th, 1966, as the document stated – but that I could not, for the life of me, remember? My handwritten initials in my own academically-correct style were at the bottom. Names appeared – State Troopers, FBI agents, a stenographer, and a doctor – but not my father, who surely should have been present for his underage daughter, in lieu of a lawyer we couldn't afford.

The document is nearly thirty typewritten pages long, and the pages are numbered from 70-plus to just over 100, not 1 to 20-something. A complaint in the introductory paragraph said that it could not be done until the 19th because the doctor wouldn't allow access to me on the day I'd been admitted to the hospital.

How many hours does it take to interrogate a witness for twenty-odd pages of coherent, orderly narrative with acceptable grammar, given that it wanders in and out of an accent I don't quite speak? It must have taken hours, if not an entire day. Someone had wanted me to do that the very day I was rescued – before the hospital staff had even had time to observe my condition for half a day or let me finally sleep after the week-long ordeal.

I didn't remember a minute of any such interview that day, or any day.

And it was wrong, all wrong. I wouldn't have said such things. If I was going to perjure myself like that, I'd certainly have made myself look better. I would never, ever have made that very sick and violent murderer, William Hollenbaugh, into the comparatively chatty, informative, affectionate, even almost romantic figure that appeared in those pages.

All the same, apparently it became the Word. I've since seen some of the headlines and articles in scrapbooks and preserved material. The papers, and then the magazines, from that day for as long as the stories appeared, enthusiastically passed around tales about how I'd used my "feminine guile" to fend off his romantic attentions, or how I endured them; the consideration and care he'd taken of me and his dogs; and all the details of what he'd taught me about surviving in the woods and his plans for our future life together.

It has him teaching me what mountain laurel is, and calling it "buck laurel." I had never heard it called that; not even when our state flower featured in my Biology class project, a display of local wildflowers, a year or so before the abduction. Oddly, the first time I might have seen it called by that name is in a caption to a newspaper photo from months later, showing one of the camouflaged caves the police and I had found. But I didn't see that newspaper back then.

At one point Hollenbaugh is supposed to have told me that we'd have to escape to the "Clear Ridge Mountains." There is a Clear *Ridge* above Fort Littleton, but I have never heard of any Clear Ridge *Mountains*. He never made such a remark to me, in any case. He wouldn't have.

When "I" dropped out of the accent I was supposed to have used, it was to give astoundingly accurate details that "I" had seen or that he was supposed to have told me about his firearms and the contents of his pockets, which agree precisely with the autopsy report I didn't see until years afterward. Then, he was supposed to have admitted that he did all the crimes that the police thought he'd done (in similar words) even the ones he never actually bragged about to me.

As I was beginning this book, it took a great deal of persuasion by others and much soul-searching on my part to decide to reproduce Bicycle Pete's foul language, even as far as it appears in these pages. According to this document, I did so fifty years ago – in a way. It contains far more bad language than I ever would have repeated to unfamiliar gentlemen, but nowhere near what I heard from Hollenbaugh. I would have said only that his language was bad, and refused to repeat words that no respectable girl of seventeen, living under her parents' roof, would say (and that, for the record, I did not use myself at the time.)

By far, though, the very worst thing was that I was supposed to have freely given a detailed account of Hollenbaugh sexually molesting me. Even if what is described isn't quite rape, what does appear is disgusting enough that I could never have told my Mom about it. I could not have gotten over it, not in years. And only some forty-eight hours after the last incident "I" was supposed to have suffered, *I could calmly tell all about it to a roomful of total strangers, all men, knowing that Mom would find out? Knowing that it would be splattered all through the newspaper stories?*

Did no one writing those pages realize that to a girl raised as I was, being kissed and groped by such a man would have caused far more emotional devastation than almost anything else he could do, short of finishing the crime?

Do the press and law enforcement really expect so much of every abductee, that they compose such an intimate, candid, comprehensive account in that short a time? One that dovetails so exactly with some evidence somebody else had already found, like the firearms and canned goods, but apparently wanted to hear from me as well? One that the media will broadcast to the world?

To answer my own questions, I am convinced that they did not require it of me – although someone may have wanted to.

I could go on about it. There's a lot more. It relieves my feelings to refute the details in the account, but all that is just trivia. The simple, inescapable truth is that on the Wednesday morning I was rescued, I had been transferred from a gurney to a hospital bed. There I stayed, bedridden in a private room, boredom and all, until I was allowed into a wheelchair for less than half an hour for the TV interview that Saturday. Then it was straight back to bed. My feet were so badly blistered that the covers had to be tented over them for days. If I'd been debriefed for the hours that document would have taken, it would have taken place in my room. Neither I nor Nurse Henry remember such a thing; and neither Dr. Lorenz nor Dad could have been kept away from me there. Special Agent Finbar O'Connor's name doesn't appear in the list of attendees, and he did not leave my presence that day.

After leaving the hospital I read nothing in the newspapers except for skimming the *Saturday Evening Post* and *Life* articles, and those I found garbled and disappointing. They apparently acquired their material from that document or from our news, aside from a very few questions from the *Post* writer which weren't even about the event, only about why they wanted to run their article.

Therefore, it took over twenty-five years after the kidnapping for odd remarks and happenings to begin to make sense in light of that typewritten document and the news articles.

In the summer of 1966, as State Troopers and National Guardsmen and I searched for

Hollenbaugh's hiding places, they asked some questions that I couldn't answer. I had no idea what they were talking about when they asked about a cache found in a slab pile at a sawmill near the McKenzie's. It surprised them that I only remembered one sawmill, somewhere on the south end of Gobbler's Knob, and I hadn't seen a slab pile there. Apparently, I was supposed to have stocked this one they knew about with loads of canned goods from the McKenzie's, despite the absurd risk to Hollenbaugh of ransacking a house right beside that well-used road.

On two separate occasions while I lived in Indiana, I had the pleasure of hosting FBI Agents Hal Briner and Finbar O'Connor for dinner. One had family in Chicago and the other in Michigan, and it was our good fortune that my home was on their way. It was Hal Briner who first puzzled me with a remark about reports.

"You do know they, ah, *lie*, don't you?" he asked, looking a little uncomfortable.

"They do?"

"They do," he said. "They're going to lie so they can meet their deadlines. Don't worry about it. You're tough, you can take whatever they dish out at you."

The conversation moved on. Finbar O'Connor said much the same thing to me when he visited.

One day – it must have been about 1976 – two men stopped by my parents' house and spoke to my father. Robert "Bob" Cox had won a Pulitzer Prize for his coverage of the manhunt a decade before, and Ken Peiffer had won a prestigious press award himself for one of the best out of the myriad of pictures he'd taken documenting the event – a heart-rending photo of Tom McGinn mourning over his dog Weid. Now they were writing a book about the Mountain Man and the Terror in Shade Gap, and wanted to find out how to contact me.

For a long time I didn't understand why Dad reacted as I was told he did, but I can imagine his poker face dropping into place.

"It'll cost you," he said. "Ten thousand dollars." It's big money now; it was more then. The reporters went away unsatisfied, and the book was written anyway. It is entitled *Deadly Pursuit* and is still in print, and "Robert Cox" is the only name to appear on the cover.

It repeats the errors of ten years before and adds others, such as placing Dad at the picnic grounds and in the hunt, a pathetic, broken figure confiding to Mr. Cox and police how I'd never be able to find my way home through the countryside without a road to guide me.

Here's my question: Why would they approach my father? They had cultivated some contacts throughout the area before the abduction, but as it happened, none were in my immediate family. Dad had no idea whether they were genuine. They were reporters. The papers had been full of my wedding to Darrell and then the birth of our daughter. The articles had included his employer's name, and later recounted that we'd moved to Indiana.

If newspapermen hadn't been able to find me, might it have been because they felt that my part of the story was already available in all the detail they needed?

About thirty years later I would become acquainted with Mr. Peiffer, who told me about Dad's reaction. Dad had never been the money-grubbing sort to sell my story or my personal information that way, so it puzzled me. Eventually I realized that he might have been testing them. Dad and Mom knew better than I did the tenor of all that had been written after the abduction, and how sensationalized some of it was (especially after my rescue.) They knew how some reporters had behaved while I was recovering in the medical center and all through the rest of that summer. A major magazine had had the chance to tell my story, and hadn't even asked me any relevant questions.

Dad had no reason to trust newsmen. Mr. Cox and Mr. Peiffer apparently went away without pleading a case for telling the plain truth of the story, and Dad would have felt that his mistrust was justified.

The first script for the TV movie had seemingly been inspired by *Deadly Pursuit*. By then, Mr. Cox had passed away. The souvenir scripts, notes and photos from cast members, and the paperwork – including the twenty-plus-page "official document" – were filed away, then stored, and Al and I moved again.

Since the abduction I had given the media as little attention as possible, but with the making of the movie there was once again interest. We'd moved back to the Shade Gap area by the time the film aired, at first renting a house in Neelyton that, ironically, had once been lived in by one of William Hollenbaugh's brothers.

By that time, Mom had had to retire. She'd developed diabetes, which was much less manageable at that time, and she couldn't work anymore.

Once, I drove Dad's old brown pickup in to the post office to get the mail. As I parked around the side, Mr. Leirwyn Montague, the postmaster, strode out and had me put a coat over my head, hurried me in the back way, and then had me look out the front window. A car had been staking out the front door for hours, he told me, and the driver was taking pictures of any woman of the right age who went in the door. I hung around inside until the car left.

Nonetheless, because of the movie I was granted one of the most rewarding experiences of my adult life: a visit to Oprah Winfrey's show, where other survivors of captivity in addition to myself spoke of our experiences. The show was taped on the first of May and aired on Tuesday, May 8th, 1991 – the day after the movie showed on NBC. I found Oprah to be a most genuine and spiritual hostess. In addition to myself there were two other women, both of whom had been sexually assaulted during their ordeals, and Dr.

Lauren Brooks, a victim recovery psychologist.

It seemed to surprise many people that when we were asked about receiving counseling, I was the only one who could say that I had recovered from my experience without it. That is true. I had my family, and an excellent pastor, but counseling just wasn't a part of a hospital's services then, and an expensive private psychiatrist would have been out of the question.

Another aspect that I had experienced was raised to all of us: the tendency of people to root for you – and then to critique and nitpick your performance as if it were a scripted and choreographed fantasy. Some demand that a victim become a hero by defeating the villain and escaping, by recognizing and exploiting the smallest opportunities against a larger and stronger foe. If that doesn't happen, those same people come to see the incident as a conspiracy between victim or family and the kidnapper. I came to realize that these women had gone through that same trial. It had happened to Mom and Dad and to me, and would again.

The only other time TV cameras had focused on me like that was during that interview the Saturday after my rescue. This time I did much better, neither freezing like a deer in headlights nor needing anyone to speak for me.

Our brief visit to Chicago went smoothly, despite the usual setbacks attending any long trip with a small grandson. Although, the less said about the speedy limo ride from Pittsburgh back home, the better. The driver seemed to have had a date in Ohio that evening.

As I said, by the week in which we went to Chicago and the movie aired, Al and I had settled back in the Shade Gap area.

For a while I worked as a night custodian at Southern Huntingdon High School. Cleaning toilets at your alma mater is not the most impressive-sounding job, but it was good to work at my own pace in a quiet building for a good boss. From there I moved on to Shade Gap Elementary as an aide in the special education classes, while also putting in hours at the Shade Gap senior center.

It was the senior center that led to the next position. The Area Agency on Aging called me about an office job in Huntingdon. It was better money than I was making at the time, and we had rented a nice house and Mom had moved in with us, so I accepted. I worked nearly twenty years there before I retired.

It was the kind of job that deserves its own book, for both the good things and the bad. For instance, I was proud to be involved with swimming classes. I did the legwork, asking only my supervisor's support. For a few years, the seniors could swim in the Huntingdon Area Middle School's pool. The County Commissioners came through with funds, we found the instructors and aides with the specialized training we needed, we had a lift to get people in and out of the water, and the pool was used in its off-hours. And the seniors benefitted, enjoying it as recreation and exercise.

One of the best things about such a job is making new friends. Many I'd never met before; others, like the retired Judge Himes, I hadn't appreciated or known well.

It was during these years that I really began to give back the blessings so lavishly bestowed upon me all my life. It hasn't always been easy, and of course it cannot be painless; but some blessings are only lent, and someday you must give them up.

Chapter 12

Carol Jean, the youngest of my siblings, had a temperament that was very like Dad's; she was impulsive, quick, adventurous, and courageous. After a battle with colon cancer, Carol refused a new treatment whose only certainty was that she would feel worse than ever. Two weeks later, on July 4th, 1997, she passed away.

Mom was never the same after that. She stayed active, she was President of the Three Springs Senior Center and enjoyed her bingo and bus trips and shopping, but she wasn't her old self. We knew when she went to Altoona Hospital nearly seven years later that it was for the last time.

A call from the hospital came for me at work on the morning of March 19th, 2004: Mom was upset and refusing her medications. Once she did that, she didn't have long. I left the office within fifteen minutes.

Mary and her husband, my brothers, and Al were already there. I went in to find Mom fretful and afraid, believing that she had signed herself into a nursing home – her greatest fear. She wanted to go home. In a few frantic hours I'd arranged everything; it was what I did at my job. I rode in the ambulance with Mom. She recognized every turn and section of road along the way, but didn't seem to feel reassured at all until she knew we were on what she called the "hooply road" south of Mapleton, headed away from any of the nursing homes in the area.

The family had gathered. There were about a dozen people there. Mom had asked for mashed potatoes and strawberries for lunch, and they were ready, but she only took a bite of each; eventually she asked that my grandson and great-niece leave the room, because she couldn't hear what the angels were saying. One hour and twenty-three minutes after she came back to her own place, the angels took Mom home.

When my husband suffered through a series of operations and infections, the doctor held little hope. "I know you like to be optimistic," he told me one evening, "but I can't be." He didn't think Al would last the night. I stayed at my husband's bedside and prayed.

In the early hours of the morning I looked out of the window into the fog. For the second time in my life I saw the shape of the man, and heard the Voice that had kept me going all those years ago in the mountains, reassuring me that everything would be all right. I blinked, and He was gone again, but only from my sight. And Al recovered.

Since the abduction, I have continually asked one question of God: Why me?

I've lived as best I could, and have always been blessed with a good life – not free of hardship and catastrophe, but never without some means of dealing with whatever came along. Being famous or notorious for something over which I had no control all those years ago never meant a free meal ticket for life, and never meant immunity from illness or death, poverty or hard work. For years after, whenever I'd visit my parents, I'd spend time back at the site of the kidnapping, sitting under the tree and trying to puzzle out the answer. Why had it happened to me? Why did a good man have to die, two good men be seriously wounded, and long before that why did another man grow so mentally ill as to think that he could just walk off with a human being? Why did my family have to suffer so much, and what was behind the massive response to the crime upon a girl and a family that so few of the responders were even acquainted with?

Eventually I made peace with the question, even if I've never quite found an answer. God apparently wanted it to be me, and I still live, and that will have to do. But when asked whether I'd go through it again, the only reply I've been able to give is: Absolutely.

Think of it: We were not only free of the Mountain Man, but there was a face and a name to put to him, and so there was closure. Dad quit drinking, my mother no longer suffered the abuse that had plagued the family, and my parents' marriage was undoubtedly saved. It all doubtless played a part in Dad's decision to accept God's salvation, and long before that, my own soul had been saved along with my life.

I had decided, during my ordeal, that I did not hate the kidnapper as much as I pitied him. Had he lived, I maintain that had I been permitted and able to do so, I would have tried to help him – although I doubt it would have been possible. One person's decision to put aside hatred may not be a big thing, but I believe that is how God wants me to live and act.

Forty-two years after the kidnapping, I faced a growing crowd. The Fulton Fall Folk Festival overwhelms McConnellsburg and extends throughout Fulton County. I'd been asked to speak at the high school one evening. I think the organizers expected a few hundred people at most, but we ended up with closer to a thousand, packing out the school auditorium and probably violating fire codes. People just kept coming and of course no one had thought that tickets or crowd control would be needed.

I spoke, and found that I could speak. I started with who I am and what had happened a long time ago, and how by the grace of God I lived to tell the story; then I answered questions. Since then I've done over three hundred such events, usually for churches, historical societies and schools. That one at McConnellsburg is the first of four that stand out for me.

Curiously, after Leap Day the dates of 2016 align with those of 1966, and May 11th was a Wednesday just as it was the day I was taken. The Huntingdon County Historical Society had originally wanted me to speak at their usual venue in the library, but had to move a few blocks away to St. James's Evangelical Lutheran Church – first to the meeting room, then to the sanctuary and overflowing into the foyer.

By then I could honestly report progress on the book I'd wanted to write for years. Afterward, as I stood at the door, people I remembered greeted me: retired State Trooper Howard Parlett, former schoolmate Sharon who dropped a little bombshell with the news that the sawed-off shotgun used by Hollenbaugh had been stolen from her father's store, Mr. Dell who reminded me of an engagement to speak at the high school. An elderly lady stood off to one side until things quieted a bit. I'd never met her before, but she introduced herself and I recognized the name of a prominent local family. When I contacted her later, she related an incident from the day before I was rescued. She'd been traveling to Harrisburg and stopped at the Path Valley Restaurant in Spring Run before getting on the Turnpike. It was so full that the waitress asked her to share her table with an FBI agent, Terry Anderson.

The night before that huge event, on Tuesday the 10th, we'd gone to Waynesboro. The Antietam Historical Association had assembled a panel consisting of its president, another member who was an historian, Ken Peiffer who had photographed the manhunt for the Chambersburg *Public Opinion*, and myself. After an excellent meal, the discussion got underway.

The first several questions were asked by a Society member, and then it was opened to the floor. I hope to do something like that again. Being on a panel was tremendous fun, even down to playing *that song* again.

The last of the four events that I consider especially meaningful was held outdoors on a rainy morning at the Cumberland County Law Enforcement Memorial in Carlisle, PA, on Tuesday May 17th – fifty years to the day after Terry Anderson's death. Similar services are held every May to commemorate those who have died in the line of duty, but this one was dedicated particularly to Agent Anderson. Somehow I spoke, although I was nearly crying; his children were there whom I'd met ten years before, as was his former partner, one of those who had asked me to come and speak. The Anderson family was presented with a flag, and then we wandered around the memorials, stopping longest at Terry Anderson's stone with its bench.

Afterward we went inside for coffee and cookies. The family took me aside into the quiet hallway, and presented me with their father's flag, saying that they already had the one from his coffin. It is currently awaiting a proper case.

I met other people there, too: one lady involved in the mental health field, and an FBI chaplain. Another man introduced himself as "the guy who was standing on the milk cans." I knew what picture he was talking about, from the newspaper fifty years before: a man cradling a rifle under his arm, balancing precariously with each foot on a separate milk can, because that was the best thing available to lift him up for a view of the fields.

Other events have led to other things. After one gathering an older lady asked me what she should do about her fear that she was being stalked. I told her to contact the police, but she had and felt that nothing had been done. She kept calling me, and I kept calling her local police department, until the day they told me that a man had been watching her house. He was arrested for loitering.

There is a gentleman from New York who was traveling in the area and was caught in traffic during the manhunt; he tries to come to an event every year. Alan Batterman's Facebook page has wonderful pictures of Shade Gap and environs through the years.

This summer, 2016, I spoke at a church, and mentioned the night I'd been forced through the stream outside Burnt Cabins, seeing one man light up a cigarette and another dummy waving a flashlight. Whatever prompted me to use such a word I don't know, but afterward a man and his family approached me. "I was the dummy with the flashlight," he introduced himself, laughing. He had wanted to meet me for years. He explained that he'd been ordered not to shut the light off. He also told me that some of the men had heard noises from the water, but hadn't known what to make of them and hadn't investigated further, just from not knowing what to look or listen for.

At the Waynesboro panel, a man introduced himself as one of the Juniata College students who had volunteered to search that weekend.

Blair Shore had photographed the manhunt for the *Daily News*. Before he passed, he came to hear me speak. He gave me advice I'd sorely needed for a long time about dealing with the press. "Remember," he said, "you never have to tell them anything. They can try to pressure you, but without you they don't have the story they came for. If they push too hard, just tell them that you're not answering any more questions. Newsmen seldom make that mistake twice."

Once a lady handed me her card. "Call me if you need anything," she said. She is now my lawyer, and on top of that knows about getting a book published.

Only once has someone been really critical. Very recently I spoke at a church, and as I greeted people afterward, a veteran maybe ten years my junior came up and said, "You did it wrong. I've heard you before." It became clear that he had been to at least two other events where I'd spoken. "You had skills. You should have taken him down and it could all have been over in hours."

He seemed to think that, at seventeen and

never having been through any combat or martial arts training, an unarmed five-foot-two girl should have escaped, or incapacitated or killed, a much stronger, armed, *prepared* man. I could thank this veteran for his service, but I could not agree with him. He refused to shake my hand.

I've mentioned some old friends already, some of whom contributed to this work. Marie Henry, my nurse from my stay at the Medical Center, came to the Fulton County Historical Society dinner in April of 2016. At ninety-five, she is still active and has a wonderful memory.

So do the former Audrey Kling and her father. One of my classmates – we are currently putting together our 50th high school class reunion – she came into the restaurant in Shade Gap one evening as we were dining, and we appointed that Thursday to go to talk to her father and sister and herself. The Klings had given William Hollenbaugh work, and they remembered him well. I'd never known Audrey to be a mimic until she gave the most unnervingly accurate portrayal of him, and then of Mrs. Ott, our Latin teacher.

Several times I've been interviewed by local news crews. Last November I showed a reporter and cameraman around the valley for an afternoon, and we pulled off the road at the Rubeck farm. There were two men with a dog across the road from the dilapidated house. I gave my name, and asked if we could shoot some video.

"I don't believe it," said the older man. "Do you know who I am?"

I didn't. It took a moment for the light to dawn. I gasped, "Are you *Mr. Rubeck*? Let me shake your hand!"

It had been forty-nine and a half years, and I'd never met Larry Rubeck. We spoke for a while. He values his privacy; we left without any pictures or an interview, and very likely I will always disagree with him on who shot Hollenbaugh. But I was so very glad to meet him, at long last.

Of course, there was the time that my grandson's class was reading *Deadly Pursuit*. When the teacher objected to Brian's criticism of the book, he asked if he could bring his grandmother to class because she'd been there at the time. I went. I think he spent the rest of the class in study hall.

Even now, I haven't read more than excerpts from *Deadly Pursuit*, nor have I ever closely read the newspapers from which "my" version of my captivity was taken. I had very little to do with it. The *Daily News* disposed of one question by stating baldly that there was no sexual assault; but after that, the fantasies were spun about me using my "feminine wiles" (the papers actually used that phrase!) to fend off my captor's romantic intentions. There seemed to be more attention paid to that subject than to anything that truly mattered. The fragile relationship between the police and many of the residents that had long discouraged confidence, or the convict who had found out how to manipulate the mental health system for long enough to achieve his release from Farview, merit much more attention.

The source for the reporters from the day following my rescue is evidently the twenty-odd page document that I've mentioned before, the one that the movie script writer sent me. It says that it's from an interview I gave for the FBI and State Police.

I'd thought it was an FBI paper, but at most a copy must have been provided to them. A former FBI agent told me firstly that their reports aren't like that; they must satisfy a much higher standard of both writing and investigation. Then he said that I would never have been deposed that way anyway since I was never charged with a Federal crime. Lastly, if it had been theirs, it would have remained confidential and inaccessible to the public and press, and to the scriptwriter. He also pointed out that whoever belonged to the names given on the first page are surely dead by now.

Were the State Police responsible for it? Some of the information must have come from their reports of the Mountain Man incidents, but in that case the implication of a deadline in the document's introduction doesn't make sense at first. The police were willing to wait until I was out of the hospital and out of school before I took them around the mountains in search of evidence. It wasn't until September 1966 that they stated to the press that they were satisfied that the abductor had been the Mountain Man and had acted alone, committing all the crimes they thought he had, an assertion I was already supposed to have heard Hollenbaugh make according to the document. But even in 1966 I'd had doubts about some cases because he had never boasted of certain ones I'd known about.

Some of the accurate facts may have come

from Agent O'Connor, to whom I'd vented when I was supposed to be sleeping just after my rescue, or perhaps I just don't remember having a few more words with someone from the FBI or the police. But, some of "my" statement was to have been made specifically to Trooper Tom Ruegg, who later drove me to school and to the county courthouse for four days. I'm sure I'd have recognized him as "the trooper from the hospital," but that first trip to school after I came home from the hospital was the first time we'd met; he said so himself at the time. Also, if I was in no shape to remember him or anyone else putting down my words for the hours on end it would have taken, why would *anything* I said that day have been reliable?

My lawyer saw the document, and noted that it was initialed rather than signed: not a legal paper in any sense. So, *why bother?*

At such a distance, unless someone who was there speaks up, maybe no one will ever know the details again for certain. Speaking for myself, I think that there may have been a great deal of pressure from the public or press, or even some level of government (maybe County or State) for an explanation of the unsolved violent crimes over the years that led to a *very* expensive week-long operation that cost two lives.

In short, some entity seems to have had an urgent interest in getting "my" story as soon as possible, and a reason for making the dry facts fit some motive on the kidnapper's part that the public would accept. Exactly how it came about, I'd naturally like to know; but there might be no one left who was there to remember.

A few days after I was supposed to have disposed of Hollenbaugh's motive by plainly calling it "love" and describing his actions to that end, the best reason that I myself could come up with was *companionship*, not love or sex. That was what I put in the statement for the Pittsburgh TV news crew. It's taken all this time for other circumstances in Hollenbaugh's life to come to light and suggest what he might really have been seeking.

In short, whatever happened that Thursday in the hospital five decades ago, I have either forgotten entirely for fifty whole years, or I was not present. I know what I think of the whole thing. I am also certain that the portrait of a kidnapper and murderer concocted that day will never do anything to improve the lot or the treatment of the mentally ill in any state-run facilities, anywhere.

I never read the newspapers back then, but I'm sure my parents did. My Mom begged me one time to *set the record straight*. Until I began to speak in public, I had no notion that most of what the public had read was so mistaken. The result is this book. It has taken over a year to get this far, and it has not been easy to remember all these events and the pain they involved.

Many people have added to this book, and some have recently passed on: my sister Mary Louise, our school bus driver Isaac Frehn, and Terry Anderson's widow. Someone recently said that Finbar O'Connor may have joined them.

How should I finish a life story that hasn't ended yet? My husband and I moved into an apartment building, since we aren't getting any younger. We keep busy. I still speak, and my calendar is filling up for next year.

So, I will say in conclusion:

Love the Lord your God with all your heart, and all your soul, and all your mind; and love your neighbor as you love yourself.

Respect the Blue, and the Service. The police

and military need your respect and support, because they will be there for you. They are themselves your family and neighbors.

Be aware of your surroundings. If you know or suspect that something is wrong, *tell someone.* The *best*-case scenario here is that it really is just you.

Do not neglect the mentally ill. I am assured by people who work in the field that nothing has changed in fifty years to improve the treatment of inmates and patients in institutions; they are still cycled through depending on their visible behavior or on the state budget. A cunning inmate can behave well for long enough to secure release, often enough by using and abusing religion. My case is unusual: normally, to be kidnapped by someone like William Diller Hollenbaugh is fatal in the end. I would be glad to go so far as Washington, DC to speak about the need for change to the mental health care system. Considering some of the people I've met, this might happen.

I hope this book achieves my goals, of honoring my Mom's wish, of raising awareness of what improperly treated mental illness can really look like, and of giving to God the honor and the glory not just for survival but for a most abundantly blessed life. It can never be a complete account of my life, of course; that is humanly impossible, and would be pointlessly unreadable and unkind. But it is as much of my story as I feel the need to tell.

Not least, this book is also a love-offering to the people of Shade Gap, and of Huntingdon and Fulton Counties, and to the thousands who came to my aid from all over or followed events as they unfolded; and of all these, it is most especially dedicated to FBI Agent Terry Ray Anderson, who gave his life seeking to save mine. To all those people who responded so wholeheartedly, most of whom did not even know who the student was who stepped off the bus that fine May afternoon fifty years ago, thank you. God bless you all.

Chapter 13:
The Kidnapper

From a conversation among Mr. Galen Kling, his daughters Audrey and Linda, Peggy Jackson, and Chris Armagost on Thursday September 8th, 2016, in addition to other sources

Sometime in 1962, a man moved into the red tarpaper cottage on Fogal's Hill, right along the road. No one knew much about him, except maybe that he'd been in prison and the state mental hospital, and a few might have known that had been turned away from a brother's door in Neelyton. He lived on public assistance and ate what he hunted, to all appearances; he didn't need much – no wife or children, no car, no steady job.

Now and again he worked for his neighbors on their farms, painting or other manual labor rather than working with the animals, walking or riding his bicycle there and back. He would hunt with them; he never shot any game that his fellow hunters recalled, though he was strong enough to carry a deer out of the woods on his shoulders instead of dragging it out as most men did.

Three dogs were soon added to his household. They were probably intended to be watchdogs. He fed them, they followed him here and there, or the smallest one might ride in the front basket of the bicycle; and that was about it. Everyone had dogs, so did Bill Hollenbaugh.

One of the farmers who employed Bill was Galen Kling. In school, Mr. Kling had learned welding; one of his classmates had been Mildred L. Moore. Then he'd gone into the Navy and served aboard the USS *Savannah* during the War. A two-year hitch as a loader and then as a director/operator on the 40mm guns ruined his hearing, but he returned home to own and run his farm north of Burnt Cabins, near the Huntingdon County line.

The valley wasn't a perfect utopia, of course.

As with anywhere else there had always been a little crime and a few criminals, petty thieves, poachers and peeping toms. In the early nineteen-sixties, however, things escalated. There were more incidents involving prowlers, a window shot out that just might have been a hunter, cars exiting the Turnpike with fresh bullet marks. Then in the spring of 1964 came the rash of attacks on women and a notable one-night crime spree in Orbisonia. The perpetrator earned names for himself: the Shade Gap Sniper, the Mountain Man.

"Who do *yeew* think's the Mountain Man?" Bill would drawl as he sat in the chair under the phone in the Kling's kitchen. "Them cops're so *dumb*," he'd go on, dropping his lower jaw as he laughed, showing the blackened stumps of his teeth. He didn't make for a pleasant visitor. To begin with, he never bathed or washed his clothes. But he had worked for the Klings off and on since he had moved into the shack on Fogal's Hill, and the man with the simple demeanor had given them no cause to refuse him hospitality. He called himself a Christian, and would quote from the Bible; entire chapters, not just Psalm 23 or the Old Hundredth, but less well-known passages, always appropriate to the conversation.

When the Klings were done with their newspapers, they would pass them on to Bill. He'd ride his bicycle to the Kling farm, leaning it up against the tree in the front yard, and maybe a dog or three would have followed him. He took to just walking into the house; once he startled Mrs. Kling, who had stepped out of the kitchen.

"*Scaaaared* ya, didn't I?" he drawled, and hooted with laughter. It was evidently the best joke he'd had all day.

For two years, the Mountain Man's activities seemed to come in spurts. There were a few incidents over those years that the police and the paper covered, and many more that they never knew about.

Among those, Stanley Locke and his wife – neighbors of the Kling's – found traces of someone sitting outside their house, just where the watcher could see into the bathroom. In Orbisonia, the wife and daughter of Mr. Houck drew the curtains against a man standing on the sidewalk one evening, in overcoat and hat, watching their house. The man left only when Mr. Houck approached on his way home from work. Another incident from 1964 never reported to the police involved a man using a ladder to access a second-floor bedroom at Guy Price's house near Neelyton, the room where his niece Peggy Bradnick was to have stayed that night.*

And still, Bill Hollenbaugh was fascinated by the Mountain Man, who could see everything and take or shoot anything and get away from the dumb cops. Among those he'd speak to, Hollenbaugh couldn't long hide his conviction that it wasn't only the cops who were dumb, because he himself was the smartest person there was on earth.

Another subject he loved to expound upon was that he'd been set up, all those years ago. The cops had been too dumb then to arrest the real burglars, and he'd spent his life locked up because of it. Then, after his release, he'd found that he'd been done out of his birthright.

The Klings could not know the full truth of the affair: that he likely had been set up by the burglars, who were other kids around his age. Because Bill had allegedly attacked his mother some little time earlier, it may have been the case that no one was keen to see him free again.

Nor could they know that he was the eldest of four children, that his father – by some accounts the only visitor that he'd spoken to in prison, by others he'd had no visitors at all – had passed away the same year that he'd been released, and that his sister still lived in Mifflintown. He was known there to other residents who saw him sitting on her porch. But if there was money or property from his parents' estate, he never displayed it.

One night, there were soft noises on the Kling's back porch, and then – further along the same wall – a sharp tap on the lighted bathroom window, startling Audrey inside. The window was too high up for even a tall man to look in, and was barely in reach for a shorter man. The next time Bill dropped by, he swore up and down that it hadn't been him; but the Klings knew better. His dogs had been wandering around the house and barn that next morning.

It wasn't lost on the Klings that Bill could well be the Mountain Man himself. At that time, though, the police weren't particularly well-respected. Dogs in the yard and a self-satisfied manner might not have been enough proof to justify the risk of setting the cops on a neighbor; it was felt that the police might regard it as an attempt to divert suspicion from those reporting their suspicions. By 1966 Hollenbaugh had already passed one lie detector test. There would have to be clear evidence before anyone spoke up.

One day in the spring of 1966, Mr. Kling was out plowing with the tractor. The children still living at home were at school. Mrs. Bernice Kling was by herself in the kitchen, ironing the laundry, when Bill Hollenbaugh walked in uninvited and stopped short.

"Where's my chair?" he asked belligerently. Mr. Kling had taken the chair under the phone, along with another one, away to be refinished. Mrs. Kling told Bill so. He wasn't listening.

"Where's my chair?" he began to shout. *"WHERE'S MY G-DDAMN CHAIR?!"*

Mrs. Kling unobtrusively unplugged the iron and moved behind the ironing board. "Bill, quiet down, you have to go out onto the porch now!" she began, trying to soothe him. But Hollenbaugh was working himself into a rage, the sort in which he might not even feel a burn or a clout from the hot iron. Her husband, she knew, would never be able to hear her voice from the house.

Somehow Mrs. Kling got him outside, and he left on his bicycle, still in a foul temper. Later that evening Galen Kling went to Bill's shack and confronted him. Among the things he said was that Bill was never to enter the Kling's house again unless he knocked and Mr. Kling answered the door personally. Bill Hollenbaugh had burnt his bridges.

According to other sources, around that time Hollenbaugh also lost patience with the assistance office, and stopped his account.

Work was proceeding on Route 522 that spring, from the county line just past the Kling farm, up to and around Shade Gap. Early in May the crews had one lane completed past the Kling's front door, concrete slabs rising a good six inches at least above the old roadbed. It slowed traffic horribly, of course, and forced detours by way of Decorum Road or Mountain Foot Road. The weather had been rainy that spring and all the streams were high; but it was a fine Wednesday afternoon when the children got off the bus.

Before dark, though, came the news that Audrey's friend and classmate Peggy Bradnick had been abducted. Immediately the Klings realized that Bill Hollenbaugh must be the prime suspect. They told the authorities so, first the firemen in their truck who were helping the police canvass the area, and then the state troopers themselves.

The first people who might have been able to provide information on Hollenbaugh's movements were his neighbors, but they were elsewhere. Emory Fogal had been in the VA hospital in Hollidaysburg since the beginning of the week, attended by his wife Kate. None of the children were staying at the farm at the time.

Ronald Fogal was a truck driver. He was traveling out of the state that week with his partner and cousin Carl Kling. Carl owned a few horses and boarded them at the Fogal farm. With the Fogal family dealing with Emory's ill health, Carl had needed someone to care for his horses while he was on the road. Despite what had happened with Carl's mother mere weeks before, Bill Hollenbaugh was nearest. He agreed with Carl to do the feeding.

Emory Fogal passed away at eight in the morning that Thursday, some sixteen hours after the kidnapping. The funeral was set for Monday, with the viewing to begin Saturday evening in Orbisonia. Those details were published that Friday, both in the *Daily News* and by WHUN, the

Huntingdon AM radio station, at 11:55 a.m. Ron and Carl got the call in St. Louis; they left their truck there and flew in to Pittsburgh.

"Hey, how about that kidnapping in Pennsylvania?" commented the cabbie on the way to the airport. "Someplace called Shade Gap." Maddeningly, there was no more specific information until Ron's sister Margaret picked them up at the airport in Pittsburgh.

It was now Saturday, and the family had descended upon the Fogal farm. When they realized that the animals had been neglected, Lloyd and Blanche Fogal drove back to Shade Gap to get Andy Locke to care for them while the others got ready for the viewing.**

When Ron and Carl arrived, Carl immediately went to see his horses while Ron went to confront Hollenbaugh. The cabin was deserted except for the dogs locked inside. The horse feed hadn't been touched before that afternoon, so Carl and Andy could work out exactly how long it had been since anyone had fed the horses. It was enough for Ron to call the State Police.

The police had already been keeping an eye on the cabin. Still, the farm was once again deserted around dusk: the whole family was in Orbisonia at the funeral home. The troopers staking out the cabin might have heard a shotgun going off. One of them, investigating the side of the shack that faced away from the road, saw two figures disappearing into the woods.

The next evening, a house was broken into. The subsequent discovery of a stock of canned goods in a nearby slab pile was no doubt correctly attributed to the Mountain Man, but despite reports, the loot had not all come from that single incident. Among other things from other places there were jars of jelly canned by Mrs. Kling, that had been stored in the Kling's basement and pilfered over some time.

The Klings were devastated by the kidnapping. The Bradnicks were friends. Not only had Mr. Kling been a classmate of Mildred Bradnick, but Gene came over to help when the Klings did their butchering, and of course Audrey and Peggy were friends and in the same high school classes.

But they couldn't do much to help. The Kling farm was under guard, since Hollenbaugh knew it so well; it was a logical place for him to try to hole up, if not contact the family or even take them hostage. Each morning, the bus stopped, and the children left for school days that were anything but normal.

Tuesday was the fourth such school day, until Audrey Kling was pulled out of Mrs. Ott's Latin class that afternoon.

"There's been a shooting," the Kling children were told. "Your family is all right. Your parents have given permission for you to ride the bus home." So, at the usual time, their bus departed, and arrived at the farm; but this time it was escorted by police cruisers fore and aft.

The shooting had been the murder of FBI Agent Terry Anderson. That morning, he and Trooper George Plafcan, Tom McGinn, and another dog handler from New York had set off from Hollenbaugh's cabin, guided by Lloyd Fogal whose father had been buried the day before, and who was now heir to the property. Hollenbaugh's small dog had shown up, and it was thought that he might put the tracking dogs on the trail. That trail had led nearly to Mountain Foot Road, to a logging road and a clearing just over a hill from the Kling and Fogal farms.

That evening, the Kling girls counted forty-eight police cruisers passing their farmhouse on the new side of the highway, each car laden with four troopers. Others would have come over from Path Valley or via 522 to Burnt Cabins, or by the Turnpike to Fort Littleton. The intent was to cordon off Gobbler's Knob with a chain of cars, lights, and men stretching from just south of the Kling's almost to Fort Littleton, and back around to the north.

It might have worked, but even if Hollenbaugh noticed it, his victim did not. His course went up to the summit of Gobbler's Knob that day, and then meandered down its south face that night, rather than staying in the woods and fields of the valley or finding a place to hide for the night. He stopped for breath for a few minutes at a sawmill, that was all. Then came the luck of a car and a driver at a solitary cabin, and the end of his days at the Rubeck farm.

Handcuffed to a gurney in an ambulance and escorted by a helicopter, Hollenbaugh was pronounced dead on arrival at the Fulton County Medical Center at 7:45 a.m., Wednesday May 18th, 1966. To this day, Trooper Grant Mixell is credited with shooting the Mountain Man, and to this day the coroner's report with its witnesses is disputed: could a .38 special roundnose bullet really produce the wound that killed William Diller Hollenbaugh? Mixell fired the last shot, but might it have come seconds before from Bodine? Or was the damage visible at Hollenbaugh's neck the result of Larry Rubeck's 12-gauge slug, and did the police claim the credit to prevent a fifteen-year-old boy from facing murder charges? No inquest was ever held, nor was any bullet found.

Hollenbaugh's unclaimed body was eventually buried that Saturday alongside his parents. His shack was investigated, his possessions rooted out and confiscated, his dogs adopted out to good homes. Some of his property went to the Pennsylvania State Police museum in Hershey. The tarpaper shack became a target for sightseers, thrill-seeking children or outright vandals. It still stood into the 1970's, but has since been taken down.

Where the authorities most underestimated the Mountain Man during the abduction was his speed and endurance. No one except his victim understood that he never stopped or slept to speak of. Nor could his motives be understood: it was naturally assumed, after his victimizing women for years, that the kidnapping was a rape case, when no ransom demand ever appeared.

But it wasn't. Knowing Hollenbaugh as they had, that fact did not surprise the Klings. Peggy Bradnick was as mystified as anyone. The only goal the captor had ever mentioned was impossible: a car for the Turnpike, to get to Mifflin or Mifflintown, two boroughs separated only by the Juniata River. Their best access to the Turnpike are interchanges some fifty miles or more distant by car, near Harrisburg, Willow Hill, and Fort Littleton. The abduction took place within a few miles of the latter two interchanges.

It is probable that the police felt that Hollenbaugh would try to break into the Rubeck house during that final shootout, for refuge and hostages. Peggy knew differently. He died within sight of his Golden Egg, as he called it; trying to run to the Turnpike, just across a field from the house. He never explained his obsession with his Golden Egg, the new, beautiful road that he may have known from the pictures on the free roadmaps passed out in service stations, as well as from observation. Did he think it was magical, that it could take him anywhere? Even to his old home, to which he knew it did not run, and which he could have reached within two days on foot at the pace he set with his captive?

The autopsy found a tobacco can in his pocket containing just over two hundred dollars. He would have reached Mifflintown with a car, a driver, guns, and money, and having outsmarted the stupid police. When he'd gone to prison before the War, chauffeured cars, servants, and cash in hand were the marks of the wealthy. Add guns, violent crimes, and notoriety, and the speed of the new Turnpike, and the image might become one to impress even the men he had been incarcerated with. Perhaps, he meant to take a magical road home to claim the birthright of an eldest son and heir, and woe to anyone who resisted him.

But that is all speculation; no one will ever know for certain. He never told the Klings, or Peggy. Even the lost lard can where he stashed a pistol on a cushion of papers might not hold an answer.

When the newspapers first got hold of Hollenbaugh's identity, there was a lot of misinformation flying around; for starters, he was born in Huntingdon, Mifflin, Juniata, or Perry County, depending upon which day the article appeared.

The bare facts are these: he was born William Diller Hollenbaugh on July 24, 1921, in

Milford Township, Juniata County. This isn't far from Mifflintown, and the location given in the 1930 and 1940 census records seems to be right along Route 35, but is specifically said not to be a farm. He seems to have lived in the same house with his family all those years, a low-cost rental compared to nearby households in that section of the census record. Some sort of mental illness is said to have run in the family, but specific details are elusive.

Precise information is given to the taker of the 1930 census, when Bill was nine years old. In April 1940, he was still listed in the same household but the best that could be recorded was that he was born "about 1922," was eighteen, and had a seventh-grade education. His occupation was listed as a laborer earning two hundred dollars over twenty weeks for that year. When he was convicted of the burglary, he was sent to prison. He spent the last thirteen years of his sentence at the Pennsylvania state mental institution of Farview, now Waymart. He escaped once, at an early point during his incarceration, but was eventually recaptured.

Life for the Klings settled down swiftly, and moved on. Road work resumed outside the front door. For many years thereafter two hogs would be butchered on Thanksgiving morning, a family gathering and local landmark, and Gene Bradnick would come by to help.

---

*Speculation continues as to whether there was a second perpetrator, either an accomplice or a separate actor. Some of the five canon incidents before Peggy Bradnick's kidnapping, for instance, were never mentioned by the kidnapper to Peggy and could be seen as out of character for Bill Hollenbaugh. A careful reading of Robert Cox's Deadly Pursuit *makes clear that he at least suspected a second person.*

**Parts of State Police reports quoted in other publications say that Lloyd and Blanche Fogal had been contacted by the police about Hollenbaugh's absence well before the return of Ron Fogal and Carl Kling, and that the cabin had been broken into in the fear that Hollenbaugh was ill or dead inside; and that only afterward was Hollenbaugh considered the prime suspect.

Chapter 14:

In Memoriam

On October 16th, 2006, a dream long anticipated came to pass, with the dedication of a memorial to a man who died in the service of others. What could I, or anyone, say to his family in this situation, when it was because of me?

I had never met FBI Special Agent Terry Ray Anderson, of course; I had been present when he was murdered, that was all, and no one should ever have to witness and remember such a sight. His children came to the ceremony, and I had no idea what they would think of meeting the survivor of the case in which their father had been killed. On the other hand, I had already met his former partner, retired FBI Special Agent Brinkley, one of the many who had been determined first to have a memorial marker made, and then to find a suitable location for it. That, in itself, had taken the longest time.

The marker is in the standard shape and appearance of roadside historical signs, but there had been some issues about putting it nearer the site of the shooting. Placing it along the former Mountain Foot Road was hardly practical. No one would get to see it unless they searched, and knew where to look.

After some years, the Shade Gap Presbyterian Church offered a spot right by US 522, in their cemetery. It is just across the highway from Harper Memorial Park, the headquarters of the manhunt, and there's plenty of room by the marker to pull off and see it up close. The congregation had played their part during my abduction. My own church had held an all-night prayer meeting. The Presbyterians, with their building so close to the hordes of people who had come to help, had kept their church open twenty-four hours a day, every day until the end; and they'd put together a schedule so that there was always somebody there praying. Prayer had as much to do with my survival as anything. I've never doubted that.

The FBI website has a brief biography of each agent killed in the line of duty. Special Agent Anderson's records that he was born in Iowa in 1924, and that he served in the Marines for two years during the War, achieving the rank of Lieutenant; from there he went on to graduate from Drake University and teach high school history. According to other sources he handled dogs during his enlistment, and coached football during his teaching career. An older brother had joined the FBI; so eventually did Terry Anderson. From assignments in Ohio and Philadelphia he moved to Harrisburg as a resident agent. The year before the kidnapping, he traveled to Huntingdon to speak at the Good Scout banquet, and so was known to county residents.

One of his sons, himself a retired FBI agent, once told me that his father could be his own worst enemy. That he was driven and focused, aggressive and sure of himself, may have resulted in the few seconds of incaution in which I saw him – as did William Hollenbaugh. Perhaps Special Agent Anderson underestimated the man he was after, assuming him to be a criminal capable of reasonable behavior and restraint when in his own interest, when the true situation was closer to facing a cornered enemy in wartime. But then, probably nobody but the Fogals and the Klings could have given him an inkling of the truth. Even they hadn't seen him as I knew him. Nobody beforehand seems to have considered him capable of being so impulsive and violent for so long a time, especially the staff at Farview whom he spent years deceiving. The police and FBI would have been working from information forwarded from there, as well as that of the local State Troopers who had had contact with the simple, strange recluse, Bicycle Pete.

And so Terry Anderson died in the line of duty, brought down not by a sniper's bullet in a deliberate ambush, but by double-ought buckshot from a few yards away by a man he had come too close to finding. The date was May 17th; in less than twenty-four hours the murderer was dead himself.

Anderson's partner Ron Brinkley was on the road when he was informed via radio of the murder. To him fell the task of informing Mrs. Anderson of her husband's death, which left her a widow with four children. The family took their father and husband home to Iowa for burial while I was still in the hospital. The papers said that he was laid to rest on Saturday, May 21st, 1966.

For all that I can admire the man I never met, the sad truth is that there is not much I can say about him. From all I've ever heard, he led a busy, colorful life, well worth a story of his own; but that should be left to others, I think, who were privileged to know him far better.

Mrs. Anderson could not attend the dedication of the Shade Gap memorial, but the children did. I need not have feared. They did not resent me for their father's death; instead, we have become good friends. I last saw them at another service honoring their father, this spring at the Cumberland County Law Enforcement Memorial. Their mother was too unwell to attend, and has since passed on. A flag was presented to his children at that service, which they in turn presented to me, in honor of my hero.

Author's Notes

The course of my duties brought me into the company of Mrs. Mary Moore. As we spoke one day, she mentioned that her sister was expected to drop by that morning. Did I know Peggy Jackson? No? Peggy Logan?

Still didn't ring a bell.

"Peggy Ann Bradnick?"

Ah.

In 1976 I was in a sixth-grade class with a teacher who made sure that we were acquainted with Current Events. One day that spring, perhaps even the second week of May, he raised the subject of the Shade Gap kidnapping and the Mountain Man.

It was an unusually active discussion for news that had happened when we were toddlers. Hunters reputedly were still finding his hideaways in the woods. Even at that age, some of my classmates knew details from people involved, either relatives or friends or neighbors. One student brought in a 45 rpm record the next day. We listened to Russ Edwards sing "Eight Days at Shade-y Gap," and we discussed the distortion of news for artistic purposes.

When I told my Mom what we'd discussed, she took me around to see the sites the next time we went to visit my grandparents in Fannettsburg. By that time, I think, Bicycle Pete's shack was gone, or would be within a few years.

Before that, I had only an inkling that something had happened. Dad would point out the car window, or the adults might shut up and change the subject when the small girl entered the room. Once a teacher had mentioned it, though, it seems I was old enough to know.

By then, Peggy had long since moved out to Indiana with her husband, and that was the latest thing anyone knew in my class.

I moved away for school and moved back home to work, and a few years later came the TV movie *Cry in the Wild: The Taking of Peggy Ann.* By that time, I'd read Robert Cox's *Deadly Pursuit.* The movie contained the points I remembered: the attacks beforehand, the abduction, the huge manhunt, the Mountain Man in a shootout that didn't give Larry Rubeck his due. The newspaper reviews were mixed, of course. To be sure, no one involved would have been impressed with anything less than a thorough and accurate documentary series. If I'd read the paper closely, though, I'd have figured out that Peggy was living back here again, but I had to go to work that day.

So, it was another twenty-odd years until we met. I'd probably seen her around, of course, just not been introduced.

That first time we met, we all ended up discussing tabletop grills. The next time I saw Peggy, she was waiting for an important call, after which things would be busy. She asked if I knew anyone who could write.

"I can write," I said cautiously, "but I've never been published." I had my Bachelor's in English Lit and I'd done a few longer fanfiction works with which I was satisfied: hardly an impressive *resume.* Before I left, I admonished Peggy not to engage a writer without knowing whether he or she could construct a sentence. I realized afterward that I knew a few newspaper reporters, as well, and passed their names along to her; but when she was ready to start her project that fall, she liked what I did.

That was good. I had to scrap everything I thought I knew about the case, and the more I found out, the more appalled I became at her treatment after the event was over, which ironically and incorrectly might have been considered kind and tactful toward the victim. As it is, the portrait of a mentally ill kidnapper and murderer from the news articles of that time is far from the truth needed to promote reform. One of Peggy's goals with this work is to correct those impressions.

Another goal is to answer questions that she faces from nearly every audience. It seems to have surprised and gratified her that so many were concerned about how she'd gotten along since moving away all those years ago.

Places and Names

As not all of the places and features in this work are named per the current maps, a few notes are in order.

Firstly, there were what the inhabitants or, in this case, the natives and then the English-speaking or German-speaking settlers called things. Then the mapmakers came through and changed a few things. Just a few years ago, 911 came through and changed things again.

Confusion ensued with the mapping of Peggy's route. The tallest point in Shade Valley is at the southern end, a rare conical peak denoted Sidney's Knob; it's a landmark for residents and Turnpike drivers alike. A few miles away, Shade Mountain ends in Gobbler's Knob. Those designations are used in this book, and can be seen on a map. But to Peggy and many residents of this part of Huntingdon and Fulton Counties, the tall pointy peak is Gobbler's Knob and the south end of Shade Mountain is the south end of Shade Mountain, somewhat split off from the rest by a pass called Pott's Gap. This confusion can be detected in newspaper accounts of the time.

The road where the Mountain Man kidnapped Peggy is now Hollow Road, but fifty years ago it didn't seem to have a formal name at all. Then, it was just a lane connecting two other roads coming south from Neelyton Road with Pleasant Hill Road. There's nothing but woods for half a mile and more north from the bus stop, except for power lines skipping over the hollow from pylons atop the ridges on each side, until the small house (not a farmhouse) rented by the Bradnicks at the time comes into view.

Decorum Road runs from Neelyton south through the tiny village of Decorum and ends at Burnt Cabins. Historically, it has also been Dry Run Hollow Road (as in PSP Trooper Plafcan's reports), Mountain Foot Road East, and Alternate 522 – since traffic was detoured that way during the road construction that took place in 1966. Dry Run Hollow itself was the Bradnicks' Mushroom Hollow. Somebody's put a house in there since.

A few years ago, 911 changed the name of Mountain Foot Road, at the base of Shade Mountain, to Tannery Road. Granted, "Mountain Foot Road" is a popular name, and there was more than one in Huntingdon County.

Mountains here are in the form of long ridges often spanning several counties. The two in this account are Shade Mountain and Tuscarora Mountain. Shade Mountain on the west is straightforward. Tuscarora to the east, pierced by the Turnpike tunnel of that name, is an example of another habit of nomenclature: the long ridges are broken up into sections, named after the towns at their feet where a road crosses over. Therefore, the residents of Shade Valley call their section Neelyton Mountain. Where the road crosses from Burnt Cabins to Fannettsburg in Path Valley, Franklin County, some might call it Fannettsburg Mountain. It all depends on where you are and who you ask.

In short, most things named are to be found on a current map or Google Earth, except for Neelyton Mountain and Mountain Foot Road. But if you ever find yourself there without knowing the area, take a detailed paper map. There might be no signal for internet or phone.

In other matters, there are only a few newspapers regularly referred to. *The Daily News* mostly serves Huntingdon County; the *Public Opinion* is from Chambersburg in Franklin County. *Southern Huntingdon County School*

District and its high school are commonly abbreviated to *Southern*.

An historical marker proclaims the water gap outside the town of Shade Gap to be the "Shadow of Death" and states that "its local significance is now unknown." The phrase is of course from the 23rd Psalm, and a glance uphill convinces me personally that a traveler moving at a walking pace along the stream had much to fear from highway robbery as well as from shifting rocks and deadfall trees. Whether the name refers to a specific incident is what no one seems to have remembered. As for the name "Shade Gap," one of Jane Austen's characters uses the word "shades" to refer to "woods" over two hundred years ago. Just a thought.

Finally, to anyone from elsewhere wishing to appreciate just what Peggy Bradnick and the searchers experienced: Beware the flora, fauna, geography, and the "No Trespassing" signs. Be respectful toward the land and courteous to the people, and bring good boots and dry socks. Watch for snakes, and check the forecast. The park at Cowan's Gap and the Tuscarora Trail might be good places to start.

Acknowledgements:

Many, many people contributed material, time, effort, and encouragement to this book, and to anyone whose name should have appeared but doesn't, we apologize now.

Editorial assistance:
Leslie Armagost
Jesse Thomas

Interviews, statements, answers, photographs, scrapbooks, prayers, and encouragement:
The family of Terry Ray Anderson, FBI
Shirley Bair
Debbie Bradnick
Ron Brinkley, FBI (retired)
Todd Dorsett
Isaac Frehn (now deceased)
Marie Henry, RN (retired)
Nin Hiles
Galen Kling and family
Alicia Marie Logan
Jean McMullen
Howard Parlett, PSP (retired)

Ken Peiffer

Sharon Querry

Our especial appreciation goes to Mrs. Sandy Kleckner, who made her father's collection of photographs available to us: Mr. Blair Shore was for many years a photographer for *The Daily News* of Huntingdon, PA.

Jayne Garver, lawyer, has been instrumental in the production of this book, from knowing how to use CreateSpace to sorting out contracts and paperwork at the birth of Mountain Voices, LLC – as well as coming up with that name. Thank you so much!

Also, we wish to thank Mr. Lloyd Dell, who agreed to write us an introduction. His involvement in so many aspects of the case gives him a unique perspective of the entire course of events.

The map is the 1944 shaded edition of the United States Department of the Interior's Geological Survey of 1939, used courtesy of PASDA (PASDA.org.) One of the reasons it was chosen is that the shading gives a powerful impression of the rugged landscape faced by Peggy and the searchers. Another reason is that it depicts the roads, especially US 522, as they were at the time, twisting and turning with the landscape; although I doubt that anything could fully convey the frustration added to the situation by a highway under construction. There is a picture included in the book of a barn with an advertisement painted on its side: the vehicles are using the unfinished roadbed. Some five miles north of that spot, all traffic had to go through Shade Gap rather than around.

We also wish to thank the PA State Police Museum, *aka* the Heritage, Education and Memorial Center (psp-hemc.org) and its curator Meagan Walborn, who passed along some information about their Mountain Man exhibit that we hadn't known. We thank all of you.

Chris Armagost

Any note of appreciation on my part must start with my husband Al, my daughter Alicia, and my grandson Brian and granddaughter-in-law Gina. Beyond that, where can I begin? There has been so much support for this book from everyone, family and friends, from all over the area and beyond. Thank you all! I don't know what else there is to say.

Peggy Jackson

Made in United States
North Haven, CT
22 October 2022